OSPREY AIRCRAFT OF THE ACES • 107

Soviet Hurricane Aces of World War 2

10

SERIES EDITOR: TONY HOLMES

OSPREY AIRCRAFT OF THE ACES • 107

Soviet Hurricane Aces of World War 2

Yuriy Rybin

OSPREY
PUBLISHING

Front Cover
During the short polar day of 15 December 1941, when it was only light between 1100 hrs and 1400 hrs, 11 Hurricanes of 78th IAP of the Northern Fleet Air Force took off in two groups to escort six twin-engined bombers – two DB-4Fs and four SBs – whose crews had been ordered to attack enemy frontline positions.

Following the failure of the Wehrmacht's September advance on Murmansk, *Gebirgsjäger* units were digging in for a lengthy period of 'trench warfare', but their activities were being disrupted by Northern Fleet aircraft, which were systematically bombing their positions by day and night. Cloud cover was, in places, down as low as 600 m (1950 ft), yet the influence of the gulfstream kept the air temperature on the northern shores of the Kola Peninsula relatively warm. It was about -10°C, even though in more southerly areas of the northern front the temperature was down to about -25°C.

The Soviet aircraft dropped their ordnance during their first run, and they were followed over the target by 11 Hurricanes carrying bombs on external racks. The latter dropped 34 2.5 kg (5.5 lb) bombs plus 1000 leaflets. As soon as the Soviet formation had set course for home, Bf 109Es of 14./JG 77, led by ace Leutnant Alfred Jakobi, appeared from out of the darkness at high altitude. The interception did not come as a surprise to the Soviet pilots, however, and two formations of Hurricane IIs, led by Lts Dmitriy Amosov and Konstantin Kononov, quickly turned to meet the German attack.

At first the Soviet aircraft remained in a cohesive group, but this soon broke up when individual dogfights started and each pilot ended up on his own. This was due to the Soviet reliance on a basic fighter formation that consisted of three aircraft, rather than a pair as was the case with other Allied and Axis air arms. The former proved impossible to keep together during combat manoeuvres. The Germans immediately shot one Hurricane down when it separated from the main formation, the aircraft crashing in flames in enemy-held territory and its pilot, Lt K G Kononov, being killed. Two other Hurricanes sustained combat damage but were able to return to base.

During this brief battle Lt Amosov, flying Hurricane IIB Z3768 adorned with the legend 'For the All-Union Communist Party of Bolsheviks (VKPb)', managed to fire a long burst from all 12 of his Browning machine guns at a Bf 109 from a range of 70-100 m (75-110 yards). According to the pilot's report, the Messerschmitt crashed in enemy territory and exploded. This was the first victory scored by Dmitriy Amosov in a Hurricane, the future ace having claimed his first kill on 23 August 1941 while at the controls of an I-153 biplane.

Z3768 remained Amosov's mount until it was written off in combat on 31 August 1942, by which time he had taken his score to seven victories, including five achieved whilst flying a Hurricane II (*Cover artwork by Mark Postlethwaite*)

First published in Great Britain in 2012 by Osprey Publishing
Midland House, West Way, Botley, Oxford, OX2 0PH
44-02 23rd Street, Suite 219, Long Island City, NY, 11101, USA

E-mail: info@ospreypublishing.com

Osprey Publishing is part of the Osprey Group

A CIP catalogue record for this book is available from the British Library

ISBN: 978 1 84908 741 4
e-book ISBN: 978 1 84908 742 1
e-Pub ISBN: 978 1 78096 885 8

Edited by Bruce Hales-Dutton and Tony Holmes
Page design by Tony Truscott
Cover artwork by Mark Postlethwaite
Aircraft profiles and line artwork by Aleksander Rusinov
Originated by PDQ Digital Media Solutions
Printed and bound in China through Bookbuilders

12 13 14 15 16 10 9 8 7 6 5 4 3 2 1

Osprey Publishing is supporting the Woodland Trust, the UK's leading woodland conservation charity, by funding the dedication of trees.

www.ospreypublishing.com

CONTENTS

HURRICANES IN SOVIET SERVICE

Many books and articles have been written about the pilots who fought in the legendary Hawker Hurricane. Inevitably much of this attention has been devoted to those who distinguished themselves in the skies over Britain in 1940, and it was hardly surprising that the annual Battle of Britain flypasts over London in the immediate post-war years were led by a Hurricane.

Similarly, many words have been written about the Allied pilots who fought against Axis forces in other theatres during World War 2 while flying Hurricanes. But little research has been conducted into the exploits of the many Soviet pilots who flew the legendary fighter. What has appeared in print in the past has been fragmentary in nature and often, to put it mildly, full of inaccuracies.

Yet in 1942 the Hurricane was the most numerous Western Allied fighter in the inventory of the Soviet Union's Red Army and Naval Air Force units serving on the enormous Soviet-German front. A major expansion of Red Army Air Force fighter regiments had been made possible by the monthly shipments of equipment from the Allies under lend-lease, which had been arriving since December 1941.

In the winter of 1941-42 these shipments were needed more than ever. The halting of the German advance on Moscow in January 1942 encouraged the Soviet command to build on this achievement with a series of offensive operations along the western, northwestern and Kalinin fronts. Many of the fighter regiments equipped with the Hurricane were the first to be mobilised along these fronts. Specifically, the units involved were 1st Guards and 157th, 191st, 195th, 488th and 736th Fighter Air Regiments (*Istrebitelniy Aviapolks*, IAPs). The latter two units were air defence regiments subordinated to Moscow's 6th Air Defence Fighter Corps (*Istrebitelniy Aviakorpus,* IAK), which also boasted three more air regiments – 67th, 428th and 438th IAPs – that were equipped with Hurricanes.

During this period these regiments were typically comprised of two squadrons, each of which was equipped with 20-22 aircraft. The latter figure also included training and liaison aircraft.

This, however, was just the start of the re-equipment of Soviet fighter regiments with aircraft

Soviet Hurricane units typically operated from primitive unpaved airfields as seen here. This machine has RS-82 rocket rails fitted beneath its wings. The RS-82 was used by most Soviet fighter types during the first year of the war in the east

supplied by the Western Allies. During the first six months of 1942 new regiments were formed on the Karelian Front at an impressive rate. By the beginning of the summer 13 were equipped with Hurricanes, namely 145th, 147th, 152nd, 197th, 435th, 609th, 760th, 767th, 768th, 769th, 835th and 837th IAPs and 17th Guards Ground Attack Regiment.

It is also clear that the build-up of flight crews for such a large number of new units was mainly the result of accelerated flying training courses. Thanks to the Hurricane's relative simplicity, Soviet fighter pilots were able to familiarise themselves with their new aircraft and become operational on them fairly rapidly.

Yet the Hurricane's contribution to the Soviet war effort has tended to be overshadowed. Its performance was considered inferior to that of the Messerschmitt Bf 109Fs and Gs opposing it. Many reports from this period, when Soviet fighter units suffered heavy losses, characterised the Hurricane as obsolete, bulky and slow. It was almost considered to be a burden on the fighter units operating it. And the Hurricane was unlikely to be the mount of an ace fighter pilot. Of course, there is a grain of truth in this. It was difficult to measure the Hurricane's strengths against the latest Messerschmitt fighters, and it was hardly surprising that the more highly trained pilots tried to get themselves transferred to units operating faster and more manoeuvrable fighters at the earliest opportunity.

The highest scoring ace of the Northern Fleet Air Force, twice Hero of the Soviet Union (HSU) Boris Feoktistovich Safonov, led the first Soviet fighter air regiment equipped with Hurricanes. He flew 44 sorties between October 1941 and February 1942 with the type. Although he encountered enemy aircraft only twice during this time, on each occasion he was able to increase his personal score. He was credited with shooting down a Bf 109 and an He 111 for his 15th and 16th aerial victories. But when more modern Kittyhawk Is arrived in-theatre Safonov immediately transferred from the Hurricane to the American fighter, which, until his death in combat on 30 May 1942, enabled him to account for four more aircraft (three of these were Ju 88s downed on his final ill-fated mission).

Another reason for the negative attitude towards the Hurricane was that Soviet fighter regiments equipped with imported aircraft quickly lost their operational readiness during the intense combat of 1942. This

The appearance of the Bf 109F-4 on the Polar Front in the spring of 1942 was an unpleasant surprise for Hurricane units

was due to inadequate flying training and a lack of replacement pilots and aircraft in reserve to make good losses suffered after just two or three weeks of combat. Units had to be pulled back to the rear to be re-equipped, as a rule, with another aircraft type. It was factors such as these that left bitter memories of the Hurricane with many Soviet pilots, who flew the fighter for such a short period of time that there was no possibility of them becoming aces.

The combat history of 195th IAP is typical of regiments equipped with the Hawker fighter in 1941-42. Established at Gorelovo, near Leningrad, literally on the eve of the German invasion of the Soviet Union in June 1941, 195th IAP became part of the city's 7th IAK and went operational with the Polikarpov I-16 while it was still in the process of being formed. The regiment flew 1269 combat sorties – primarily patrols over Leningrad – between 6 July and 15 September, resulting in 147 'operational encounters' that saw air defence pilots claim 60 enemy aircraft (35 fighters, 22 bombers and three reconnaissance aircraft) destroyed for the loss of 12 I-16s.

Several pilots distinguished themselves in these aerial battles, three of whom destroyed five aircraft and became aces. Snr Lt I P Neustroev, who was awarded the title of HSU on 28 September 1943, had six individual and nine shared victories to his name – he finished the war with a total of 15 individual and 10 shared kills. Capt Vladimir Abramov had claimed five individual and ten shared victories by the time he was killed in combat on 11 September 1941. Jnr Lt V N Kharitonov was also credited with five individual and ten shared victories during this period, became a HSU on 10 February 1943 and ended the conflict with a tally of 18 individual and 16 shared victories.

In the second half of July 1941 195th IAP was pulled back from the front and sent to the city of Cherepovets. Prior to this move taking place most of the unit's technical personnel were posted to another regiment still at the front, while pilots requiring treatment for wounds sustained in battle were sent to the rear. 195th IAP was then brought back up to frontline strength with recent graduates from flying schools and groundcrews posted in from other units. It had essentially been reformed.

While based at Sokol, in the Vologodsk region, in early January 1942, 195th IAP received its first Hurricanes. After ten days' conversion training the regiment was sent with its aircraft to the Kalinin Front to join the 3rd Strike Army in a two-squadron regiment based at Andreapol airfield. 195th IAP began military operations on 13 March when it undertook defensive patrols overhead Soviet troops and local rail transport, as well as in the vicinity of its own airfield.

In ten days of action 195th IAP flew 229 operational sorties, engaged enemy aircraft on 11 occasions and claimed four Ju 88s destroyed for the loss of three pilots and six Hurricanes. By 27 March, of the

Hurricanes were delivered to the Soviet Union disassembled and packed in crates. Most of those destined for service on the Kola Peninsula arrived at Kola railway station, several kilometres south of Murmansk

15 combat-worthy Hurricanes that 195th IAP had commenced operations with just two weeks earlier, only six remained serviceable.

The regimental combat report for this period describes how bad conditions at Andreapol were in March 1942. The unit lacked any form of vehicular transport, let alone specialist trucks to heat water and engine oil and clear runways of snow. Personnel lived in dugouts, which hardly represented suitable accommodation, and supplies of food, fuel and ammunition were often disrupted. Communications with headquarters were unreliable, and the generation of sorties following requests by ground forces coming under aerial attack were so badly delayed that by the time 195th IAP Hurricanes were aloft, enemy aircraft had long since returned to the safety of their own lines.

On 1 April 195th IAP was withdrawn to be reformed, having handed its remaining Hurricanes to another regiment. In this brief period of operations the unit's pilots had flown 311 sorties and engaged in 24 aerial combats, resulting in claims for five enemy aircraft destroyed. The first of these had fallen on 21 March when two Ju 88s were shot down, one of which was attributed to Snr Lt Shcherban. The other was shared between Shcherban and Snr Lt Drozdov. The following day it was announced that two more bombers had been destroyed, one of which was credited to Shcherban while the other was shared between Shcherban, Afansyev and Burya. The fifth, and final, aircraft downed, in late March, was recorded as an 'Me 115', but it was in all likelihood a Bf 110. Its demise was credited to Zlodeev, Naydenov and Klimenko.

Considering 195th IAP's brief time at the front, and the lack of an early warning system to alert the unit of approaching enemy aircraft, it is unlikely that any of the regiment's pilots would have become aces even if they had been equipped with the most up-to-date fighters then in Soviet service. Yet 195th IAP's experience was typical of Red Army Air Force units fighting on the Soviet-German front in the first half of 1942.

It is true that there were exceptions, however. One was the protracted use of Hurricanes in the skies over the Arctic by the air forces of the Northern Fleet and on the Karelian Front (with the 7th Air Army after 10 November 1942), which saw a number of pilots score five or more kills while flying the Hawker fighter. But before recounting the combat exploits of these aviators, it is necessary to describe the way the Hurricane was characterised by the combat units in this northern sector of the Soviet-German front.

Hurricanes arrived in the Soviet Union from late 1941 as a key part of the first batch of lend-lease aircraft supplied by the Western Allies, together with Curtiss Tomahawk IIs and Kittyhawk Is and Bell P-39 Airacobras. They joined the latest generation of Soviet fighters – the LaGG-3 and Yak-1 – at a time when production of the MiG-3 had been discontinued with only a few examples surviving in combat units. All of these fighters had been designed in the mid to late 1930s and put into large-scale production shortly thereafter.

Each type had advantages and disadvantages. Although the LaGG-3 and Bell P-39 were both quite difficult to fly, the Soviet fighter's main drawback was its weight thanks to its all-wooden construction, with load bearing elements made from laminated plywood. Not only was the aircraft seriously overweight (takeoff weight was 2680 kg), its 1100 hp

M-105 engine was underpowered too. Many manoeuvres could result in a considerable loss of altitude, which meant that dogfighting below 1000 m was to be avoided at all cost. Finnish and German pilots frequently reported incidents of LaGG-3s crashing even though they had not come under fire. In addition, the fighter required a lengthy takeoff run, and had a tendency to swing to starboard.

The LaGG-3's primary shortcoming was its excessive weight. The aircraft's all-wood construction, with load-bearing components of laminated plywood, was too heavy for the fighter's low-powered M-105PF engine

The Airacobra offered superior characteristics. It was relatively forgiving to inexperienced pilots on takeoff and landing thanks to the excellent view resulting from its unique nose-wheel undercarriage. Yet there were disadvantages with the Bell machine that prevented it from being widely used in the USSR. With its mid-mounted engine located behind the cockpit, the Airacobra was not always predictable in flight. The fighter demanded precision and accuracy during manoeuvres in the vertical plane, for any loss of speed could all too easily lead to a flat spin from which it was all but impossible to recover.

In many respects the Curtiss P-40 was the mirror image of the Airacobra, being easy to fly. Indeed, it could be sluggish like the Hurricane, but with a noticeable tendency to turn as speed increased. This made flying rather more complicated, especially when approaching maximum horizontal speed, which, in any case, Soviet pilots were warned to avoid so as to conserve precious fuel and oil – both in short supply in 1941-42. The aircraft was generally stable in flight, even at slow speeds. Compared with the Airacobra, landing and takeoff seemed fairly complicated in the P-40, especially with the Tomahawk II and Kittyhawk I variants. During its landing roll the aircraft could veer sharply to the left or right, and it was even difficult to keep straight when taxiing. Accidents in Soviet service were not infrequent.

The principal drawback of the early P-40 variants, however, lay in their operational characteristics. The problem was that the first series Allison V-1710-33 engines were very sensitive to the strength of their

The Bell P-39 Airacobra had an impressive performance but was difficult to fly, and therefore unsuitable for many newly-trained Soviet pilots in 1942-43 because of their limited flying experience. These particular machines were assigned to Northern Fleet Air Force regiment 255th IAP, this regiment regularly escorting Hurricanes of 27th and 78th IAPs during 1943-44

The first Curtiss P-40s to reach the USSR were Tomahawk IIs supplied by the RAF. They proved to be demanding aircraft from a servicing standpoint, which created considerable difficulties in the primitive conditions of Soviet frontline airfields. This aircraft, AH965, was flown by ace Stepan Ridnyi of 126th IAP during the winter of 1941-42

coolant mixture, powerplants being known to fail through overheating caused by only brief periods of oil starvation. Overheated metal fragments from the camshaft bearings would find their way into the coolant and cause total engine failure. In 1942 such failures in Allison engines reached 'epidemic' proportions.

The most widely used fighter during this period was the Yak-1. Easy to fly, even by pilots with inadequate training, it had reasonable firepower with one 20 mm ShVAK cannon and two synchronised 7.62 mm ShKAS machine guns. In some units additional weaponry in the shape of six RS-82 rockets and up to 200 kg of bombs could be carried as external stores. But even this aircraft was far from perfect.

First and foremost, the Yak-1 was put into mass production before the prototypes had undergone all the necessary testing. The result was a string of serious defects. Most of the shortcomings were eventually eradicated, but the necessary remedial work continued throughout the aircraft's service career. Some defects remained unresolved. They included low critical roll-over angle, incomplete fuel feed from port and starboard tanks, oil being forced out of the breather tank and failure of the reduction gear shaft seal and other seals in the liquid cooled M-105P engine. In addition, engines constantly overheated, and together with fuel tanks and hydraulic systems, they also leaked. The windscreen was

The Yakovlev Yak-1 fighter was plagued by numerous design and production defects when it first entered service, but its major tactical shortcomings were poor range and a lack of modern radio communications equipment

vulnerable to oil contamination in flight as a result. All these defects placed an unacceptable burden on groundcrewmen in operational units.

The Yak-1's lack of a radio – RSI-4 transmitter-receivers were fitted to every tenth aircraft, the others having just a receiver – imposed a serious tactical disadvantage as well. The aircraft also had inadequate range, even when lightened beyond practical limits. These factors meant that upon encountering enemy fighters, Yak pilots were reluctant to fight and would break off combat at the earliest opportunity. That was in contrast to those flying Hurricanes or P-40s.

As far as the Hurricane's operational qualities were concerned, it is hardly surprising that they were ahead of its contemporaries in most respects. While the British aircraft had been subject to a continuous process of development since the mid-1930s, the later fighters in Soviet service, whether imported or of indigenous design, were still 'raw'. In 1942 the Yak-1, LaGG-3, P-39 and P-40 were handicapped by design and operational defects.

The Hurricane's principal drawback, however, was its lack of speed. But how important was this factor in air combat on the Soviet-German front in 1941-42? The outcome of an engagement at this early stage of the conflict was normally dictated less by outright speed and more by the tactics employed, and these depended on the technical characteristics of the participating fighters. It is, however, necessary to acknowledge that most of the principal fighters in the Red Army Air Force inventory – the Yak-1, LaGG-3 and P-40 – lagged behind their main rival, the Bf 109F, in terms of maximum speed and rate of climb. The majority of Soviet pilots rarely dared enter a climbing dogfight even in the Airacobra, which was only marginally slower than the Bf 109 both in speed and rate of climb. Therefore, irrespective of the type of aircraft they were flying, Soviet pilots usually found themselves fighting on the turn. And it was in the turn that the Hurricane enjoyed an advantage over any Bf 109.

Most combats between Soviet and German fighters in 1941-42 began with a head-on formation attack. Usually, a 'defensive circle' would then be formed in which pilots would protect the tail of the aircraft flying in front of them. They were also able to repel attacks from ahead. In a defensive circle the parameters of maximum speed and rate of climb had no practical significance. This meant that in combat with Bf 109s the Hurricane was not disadvantaged in comparison with any of the faster or more manoeuvrable fighters operated by the Red Army Air Force at that time. Firepower was often the decisive factor, and the Hurricane in Soviet service had no equal in this respect.

In fact the Hurricane, with its two 20 mm ShVAK guns and two 12.7 mm large calibre UBK machine guns producing a weight of fire of 3.84 kg (8.45 lb) per second, not only surpassed all single-engined Soviet fighters but also its German opponents. The Bf 109F, armed with just one 20 mm MG 151 cannon and two 7.92 mm MG 17 machine guns, produced a weight of fire of 1.99 kg (4.38 lbs) per second. Consequently, its pilots declined to engage Hurricanes in head-on attacks. The British fighter's sturdy construction and relative bulk also made it a stable gun platform, being able to pour a concentrated stream of fire onto its target. This feature made the aircraft a useful bomber destroyer.

From a flying perspective, the Hurricane II was the easiest aircraft to master for pilots with rudimentary training in 1941-42. Furthermore, it was not a demanding aircraft to service. These characteristics made it the most suitable fighter for the Soviet Air Force during the early war period

To sum up this analysis of the Hurricane, it was a fighter whose combat and flying characteristics enabled it to stand above its contemporaries in the Red Army Air Force inventory during the first half of 1942. Thanks to these traits, most combat reports from Soviet fighter regiments of the period highlighted the aircraft's positive combat characteristics. This, for example, came from 760th IAP of the air force on the Karelian Front;

'The positive qualities of the Hurricane are its operational characteristics both on the ground and in the air. It is simple to master, and does not require lengthy training. The fighter has an advantage over enemy aircraft in its horizontal manoeuvrability in turns, it has powerful armament (following its rearmament) and can be used effectively in air defence operations.

'However, the Hurricane's level speed is insufficient to give pilots an opportunity to pursue enemy aircraft, and either engage them or to break off combat at will. Fuel starvation during a violent pull out from a dive causes the engine to cut out, which hinders the pilot in combat. Finally, the oil and coolant systems, with their lengthy circulation runs, are bulky, and this affects the aircraft in winter and reduces combat survivability.'

Another report, from 435th IAP, reinforced the main points made by 760th IAP, noting that 'the Hurricane II is an obsolescent aircraft, large in terms of its dimensions, and with an insufficiently powerful engine. The level speed and rate of climb are low. Armour protection is insufficient and the aircraft has a tendency to nose-over. The wooden propeller wears out quickly, particularly when flying from sandy airfields'.

This report also noted that the aircraft was easy to fly and had a low landing speed. It praised the mechanism for raising and lowering the undercarriage and flaps, the cockpit design and the ability to jettison the canopy in an emergency. The gun firing mechanism and gunsight were rated as 'excellent', and the operation and locating of the radio equipment was described as 'convenient'. The engine starting mechanism was considered 'excellent' too. It added;

'The armament installed consists of two ShVAK cannon, two UB machine guns and six RS-82 rocket pylons. This represents powerful armament and provides the capability to strike any airborne target. The procedures for inspecting and repairing the armament are convenient.'

The Hurricane can therefore be described as a fighter that fully met the demands of the air war being fought in the complex circumstances of the Soviet-German front in 1942. It was simple to fly, did not require special training and was able to operate from airstrips in the field. Pilots with little training not only became rapidly familiar with the aircraft but could also fly it confidently, and were able, with the improved Soviet armament installed in the Hurricane IIB, to shoot down enemy bombers. They could also successfully engage any hostile aircraft.

ON THE KARELIAN FRONT

A total of nine regiments operated Hurricanes on the Karelian Front during the fierce clashes between Soviet fighter pilots and their Luftwaffe and Finnish counterparts in 1941-42. Yet only one of those regiments, 152nd IAP, was able to boast a solitary ace within its ranks. And Pavel Ivanovich Gavrilov can also be described as 'the forgotten ace'. Even today there is not one word in any known publication describing his exploits during a particularly difficult period of the Great Patriotic War.

Gavrilov, who had been born in Leningrad on 20 June 1918, graduated from the Tashkent Railway College after six years of study in 1938. Later that year he was accepted into the ranks of the Red Army Air Force and began his military service in the Guards' battalion of the 1st Chkalovskoe Military Aviation College. Graduating in January 1940, Gavrilov was initially posted as a junior lieutenant to 163rd Reconnaissance Air Regiment, before joining 152nd IAP.

Pavel Gavrilov claimed five victories in the Hurricane, making him the only ace on the type to serve with the Karelian Front Air Force

The latter had been established in late 1939 within the 9th Army Air Force, being based initially at Voynitsa airfield near the town of Ukhta. 152nd IAP, comprised of five squadrons (two flying the I-15bis and three the I-153), played an active role in the 'Winter War' with Finland between 9 January and 13 March 1940. Following the cessation of hostilities, the regiment's fighters operated from airfields in the Petrozavodsk, Leningrad and Arkhangelsk areas.

After the German invasion of the Soviet Union in June 1941, 152nd IAP – with its five squadrons equipped with 64 I-153s – became part of 134th Fighter Air Division (*Istrebitelnaya Aviadiviziya*, IAD), within the city of Arkhangelsk's air defence system. Based at Kegostrov airfield, it was engaged in the air defence of this vital sea port. In the absence of appropriate air observation, early warning and communication posts, there were no encounters with the enemy and, in any case, at that time the only Luftwaffe flights made in this area were by lone reconnaissance aircraft.

During the winter of 1941-42 most Soviet pilots serving on the northern front converted to the Hurricane from the I-153 biplane fighter, which had previously been in widespread service with both Red Army and Northern Fleet Air Forces

In August 1941 152nd IAP was reduced in size to just two squadrons operating 20 I-153s, its remaining three units being relinquished to allow them to serve as foundation squadron for newly formed regiments. On 17 September 152nd IAP was transferred to Sosnovets airfield on the Karelian Front, from where it was to play an active role against enemy ground forces. Its pilots reported engaging in several aerial combats that resulted in claims for the destruction of three enemy fighters (a Bf 109 and two Finnish Fokker D.XXIs) and an He 111 bomber for the loss of two I-153s.

Pavel Gavrilov was among the successful pilots, recording his first success on 27 September. Although no detailed account of this battle is available, it is known, however, that five I-153s under the command of senior political instructor Sergey Khateev strafed enemy forces in the village of Rugozero. During their return flight the Soviet pilots were attacked by nine enemy fighters, which they identified as Bf 109s. In reality the I-153s had been engaged by eight Finnish Fokker D.XXIs of LeLv 10. Two of the I-153s were shot down, Lt M N Piskunov being killed and Khateev making a successful emergency landing on a country road leading from the front. Initially it was thought that only one enemy aircraft had been destroyed in return, but once back at Sosnovets the survivors of Khateev's group reported that another D.XXI had been shot down by Gavrilov. As Soviet fighter pilots tended to be judged by their success in combat, it was not surprising that Gavrilov was promoted one rank following this action.

This map shows Karelian Front airfields (marked with a circled T symbol) that were home to Hurricane regiments in 1941-43

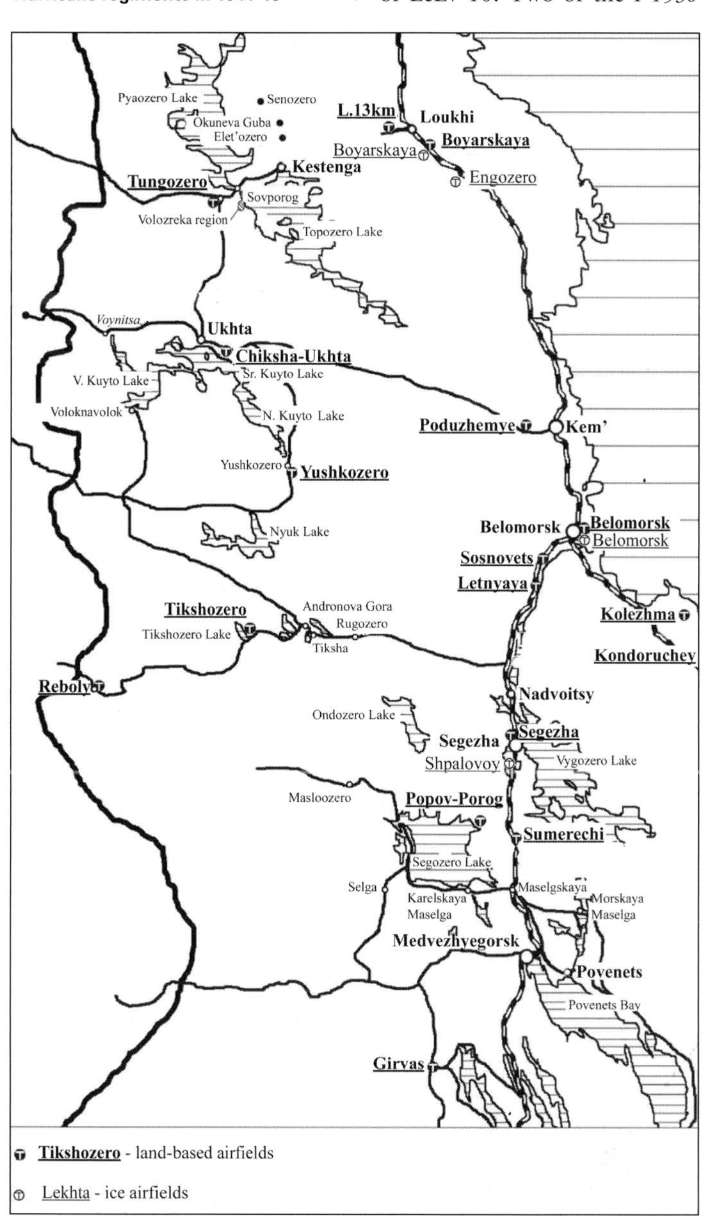

On 2 November the regiment was pulled back to a rear area outside the city of Arkhangelsk to re-equip with newly imported equipment. The Hurricane had arrived. Two weeks later, on 16 November, the regiment returned to the front with its first ten fighters. After conversion to the Hurricane, 152nd IAP became part of 103rd Combined Air Division (*Smeshannaya Aviadiviziya*, SAD), which had been formed within the Red Army Air Force on the Karelian Front at the end of October. The unit was based at the Segezhsk airfield complex and given the task of defending the southern sector of the Karelian Front, specifically the areas of Medvezhegorsk, Mosalsk and Rebolsk. The principal enemy in this sector was the Finnish Air Force.

The regiment's pilots flew their first combat sorties with the Hurricane on the day the division was redeployed to Letnyaya airfield, a pair of fighters scrambling to intercept enemy aircraft. No encounter took place, however. According to the *Journal of Enemy Aircraft Destroyed*, it was Pavel Gavrilov who claimed the regiment's first victory with the Hurricane. The journal gives the date of this initial success as 24 November, but no further information is provided.

During this period the accuracy of operational reports from 103rd SAD headquarters was seriously deficient due to poor communication with subordinate regiments, but it is surprising that a description of such a significant event is missing from the official records of 152nd IAP. Finnish sources do not shed any light on this event either, other than to point out that the Finnish Air Force did not engage in air combat that day due to poor weather. Nevertheless, it is a fact that Gavrilov scored his first individual Hurricane kill that day, the Bf 109 he claimed representing his second victory.

It should be noted that pilots from 152nd IAP converted to the new fighter with great enthusiasm since they had previously flown the low-powered, open-cockpit I-153 biplane. But as they had frontline experience, gained mainly on ground attack operations, they considered themselves fully-fledged fighter pilots, and were hungry to test themselves against enemy aircraft. At this stage of the war Soviet pilots rarely exhibited a desire to engage in active combat beyond the frontline and over enemy territory. The enthusiasm shown by 152nd's pilots to actively seek out the enemy can possibly be explained by the fact that its main opponents were units of the Finnish Air Force equipped with the obsolete Fokker D.XXI. This licence-built aircraft was inferior to the Hurricane in both performance and firepower.

During the winter of 1941-42, raids by 152nd IAP behind enemy lines were distinguished by their audacity and determination. In fact all of 103rd SAD's regiments were active despite the harsh weather. For pilots of 152nd IAP, the peak period of action was December 1941. That month Hurricanes from the regiment opened fire on Finnish aircraft on at least nine occasions, and it was reported that eight enemy aircraft had been destroyed. Pilots claimed three Bf 109s, one Brewster B-239 (the export variant of the American F2A-1 Buffalo carrier fighter), two Fokker D.XXIs and two Bristol Blenheims. Soviet losses amounted to

Finnish Fokker D.XXI fighters were inferior to the Hurricane II, and they were often easy prey for Soviet pilots (*Kari Stenman collection*)

two Hurricanes and one pilot. These combats were fought between formations that seldom numbered more than five or six aircraft.

Gavrilov increased his score on 26 December. Taking off in one of two Hurricanes scrambled to intercept a Finnish reconnaissance aircraft, he subsequently returned to report having shot down the intruding 'Blenheim', although the victory remained unconfirmed. It did, however, make him the regiment's top-scoring pilot.

Finnish Air Force Brewster B-239 Buffaloes of 2/LeLv 24 patrol the skies over Tiiksjärvi in 1942. These machines were the main opponents facing 152nd IAP pilots on the southern flank of the Karelian Front during the winter of 1941-42 (*Kari Stenman collection*)

But Gavrilov was not the only one to score that month. Squadron adjutant Lt Vladimir Basov was already a master of attacks on ground targets, his skill in this mission having seen him become one of the first in the regiment to be awarded the Order of the Red Star for his exploits. He scored his first aerial victory on 4 December in a famous action that was officially described at the time as 'a heroic chapter in the history of the Air Force on the Karelian Front'.

Three Hurricanes, led by Snr Lt Nikolay Repnikov, took off on a reconnaissance mission over Medvezhegorsk. They initially came under fire from enemy ground forces and later encountered seven Finnish fighters. The Soviet pilots identified the enemy aircraft as 'Me 109s' and 'Heinkels'. Such mistakes in aircraft recognition were not confined to the Soviet side, for the Finnish pilots involved in this engagement mistook their opponents for MiG-3s. However, to be fair to them, this was their first encounter with Soviet Hurricanes. In reality, the Finnish fighters that attacked the three machines from 152nd IAP were French-built Morane-Saulnier MS.406s from LeLv 28.

In the ensuing battle, Repnikov, in Hurricane BD761, lost his life when he rammed one of the enemy fighters (MS-329) in a head-on attack – his Finnish opponent, Sgt Toivo Tomminen, an ace with 6.5 victories to his credit, also perished. This represented the first head-on ramming attack by a Hurricane recorded in the skies over Karelia and the Arctic region. Repnikov was posthumously awarded the title of HSU on 22 February 1943. Upon their return to base Snr Lts Vladimir Basov and Stepan Ivanov each reported destroying an enemy aircraft, their victims being listed as 'Brewsters' in the official record. These kills remain unconfirmed, however.

On 29 December Basov reported destroying his second Finnish aircraft, having intercepted a 'Blenheim' on an aerial reconnaissance mission at an altitude of 5000 m (16,250 ft) while on a solo sortie after being scrambled. Following the pursuit of the enemy aircraft the oil pressure in his fighter dropped sharply and he was forced to make an emergency belly landing some distance from the airfield. In this case the Hurricane was not seriously damaged, but the destruction of Basov's victim was not confirmed.

This photograph of Hurricanes on the Karelian Front was taken in the polar twilight during the winter of 1941-42. Note the crudely over-painted RAF roundel and the red star with a black outline on the underside of the Hurricane's port wing

103rd SAD's activities concerned the Finnish Air Force command enough to force it to transfer 2/LeLv 24, equipped with Brewster B-239s, to the northerly airfield of Tiliksjarvi on 8 January 1942 to bolster the forces opposing Soviet air regiments in the area. The next day eight Brewsters were transferred from Kondogoli to Tiliksjarvi, and they encountered Hurricanes from 152nd IAP when they targeted their airfield shortly after arrival. Five Hurricanes carried out the attack, and judging by their combat reports the pilots achieved considerable success, claiming the destruction of seven enemy aircraft in the air and on the ground. What follows is an extract from 152nd IAP's account of the day's action;

'At 1325 hrs three passes were made by five Hurricanes in an attack on the airfield at Tiliksjarvi, where five aircraft were concealed in the outskirts of the forest. As a result of the attack four Fokker aircraft were taken out of action. The second airfield, where up to ten Brewsters and Fokkers were located, was attacked at 1340 hrs, and three aircraft were damaged. Up to seven Brewsters and Fokkers appeared following this attack and engaged our fighters. As a result, three Brewster and two Fokker aircraft were damaged. Our losses amounted to one Hurricane and pilot Lyusov, who, having destroyed a Fokker, was shot down. The exact location of the crash site has not been established.

'As a result of these attacks on Tiliksjarvi and the aerial battle, seven aircraft were destroyed on the ground and in the air, our pilots making the following claims – Eliseev (one Brewster), Gavrilov (one Brewster), Lyusov (one Fokker) and Zelentsov and Kuznetsov (one Brewster each).'

It is hard to believe that the pilots achieved such a high degree of success, however, with the rifle-calibre Browning 0.303-in machine guns fitted in their Hurricanes. Moreover, the Finns confirmed that only one aircraft had been damaged on the ground. Five Brewster B-239s managed to take off during the attack and two engaged the Hurricanes, but they achieved no success because their guns jammed. The B-239s sustained minor combat damage in return – just two holes in the starboard side of one aircraft. The four Fokker D.XXIs of LeLv 14 were even luckier. Having taken off under fire from the Hurricanes, future ace Sgt Hemmo Leino destroyed one of the Soviet attackers. According to Soviet archival documents, Lt V N Lyusov failed to return from this sortie in Hurricane DR340.

Nose-overs represented a frequent mishap for Hurricane pilots while they was taxiing or landing on unpaved airfields. Such an accident usually destroyed the fighter's wooden propeller, thus leading to the Hurricane spending long periods out of service due to a shortage of replacement parts

On 4 February 1942, Lt Feodosiy Zodorozhniy of 152nd IAP was conducting an armed reconnaissance mission of enemy territory when he was jumped by Finnish fighters. Although he managed to shake off his attackers, the engine in his Hurricane (Z2585) had been damaged and Zodorozhniy was forced to belly-land the fighter. Although he escaped capture to return to his unit, Soviet fighters failed to destroy his Hurricane and it duly fell into enemy hands. Z2585 was subsequently recovered by the Finns to Tampere, where the 28 bullet holes in the fuselage and wings were repaired, the engine and propeller replaced and the Hurricane issued to the Finnish Air Force as HC-45

Following this mission Gavrilov reported accounting for two more 'Brewsters', one of which was destroyed on the ground. He was also among a group of Soviet fighter pilots credited with destroying another two Fokker D.XXIs later that month. In February the regiment's pilots fought three aerial battles with Finnish Brewsters of LeLv 24, and Vladimir Basov distinguished himself once again. On 6 February he was at the controls of one of five Hurricanes that flew a reconnaissance mission to Tiliksjarvi. Appearing suddenly over the airfield at low level, the Soviet pilots saw enemy fighters scrambling to take off. Yet the Finnish pilots were able to avoid the losses that seemed inevitable. A single Brewster was making a training flight around the airfield, and Sgt Marrti Solovaara not only broke up the Soviet attack but also damaged one of the Hurricanes, holing its main fuel tank and wounding 152nd IAP ace Lt Gavrilov in the shoulder.

The Hurricane pilots were in no hurry to leave, however, and they attacked a Fokker D.XXI that had appeared over the airfield upon its return from a combat sortie. Having 'destroyed' it, they then returned to base. The Brewsters that had been scrambled to intercept them did not pursue the Hurricanes. Lt Basov was able to add a third downed enemy aircraft (a Brewster) to his tally following this mission.

In the early months of 1942 many of 152nd IAP's pilots received the Order of the Red Star and the Red Banner for their combat successes, but only Pavel Gavrilov, now a senior lieutenant, was awarded the Soviet Union's highest honour, the Order of Lenin, which he received on 20 March. By that time he had amassed a total of five individual and three shared victories.

152nd IAP continued to see action through to April, when a sharp rise in the temperature brought the spring thaw. This rendered Letnyaya airfield inoperable as the previously compacted snow turned to mud, resulting in a brief halt in operations *(text continues on page 28)*.

The remains of Hurricane II AP588 were photographed at Poduzhemye airfield on 7 April 1942. The CO of recently formed 767th IAP, Maj L P Yuryev, took off on his first flight in a Hurricane without realising that a groundcrewman who had been sat on the tail during power runs had failed to get off prior to takeoff. Upon realising what had happened, Yuryev hastily attempted to make a turn in order to land, but the aircraft stalled and crashed due to the shift in its centre of gravity. The pilot was killed and the groundcrewman badly injured

COLOUR PLATES

1
Hurricane IIB Z5205 of No 134 Sqn, No 151 Wing, Vaenga-1, October 1941

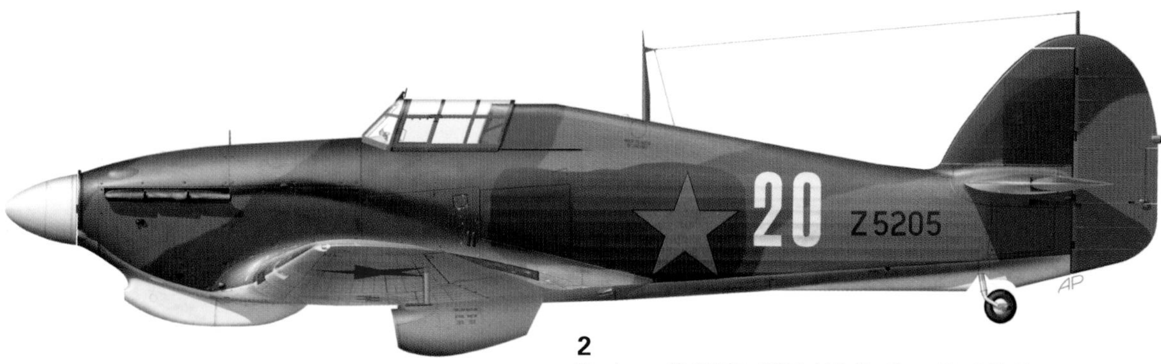

2
Hurricane IIB Z5205 of 78th IAP, Northern Fleet Air Force, Vaenga-2, late 1941

3
Hurricane IIB Z3768 of No 81 Sqn, No 151 Wing, Vaenga-1, autumn 1941

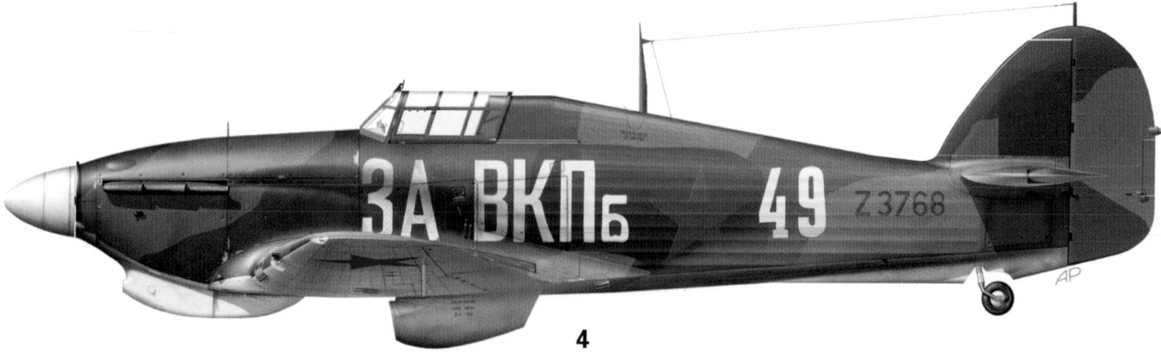

4
Hurricane IIB Z3768 of 78th IAP, Northern Fleet Air Force, Vaenga-2, 1941-42

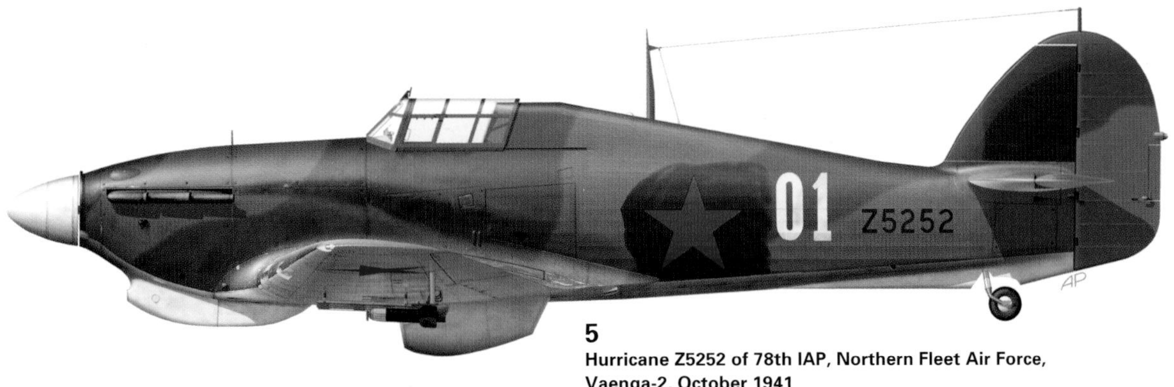

5
Hurricane Z5252 of 78th IAP, Northern Fleet Air Force, Vaenga-2, October 1941

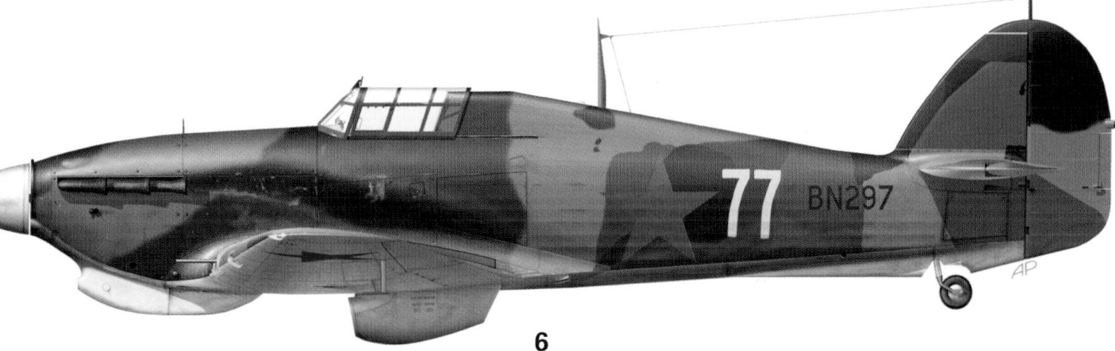

6
Hurricane IIB BN297 of 78th IAP, Northern Fleet Air Force, Vaenga-2, spring/summer 1942

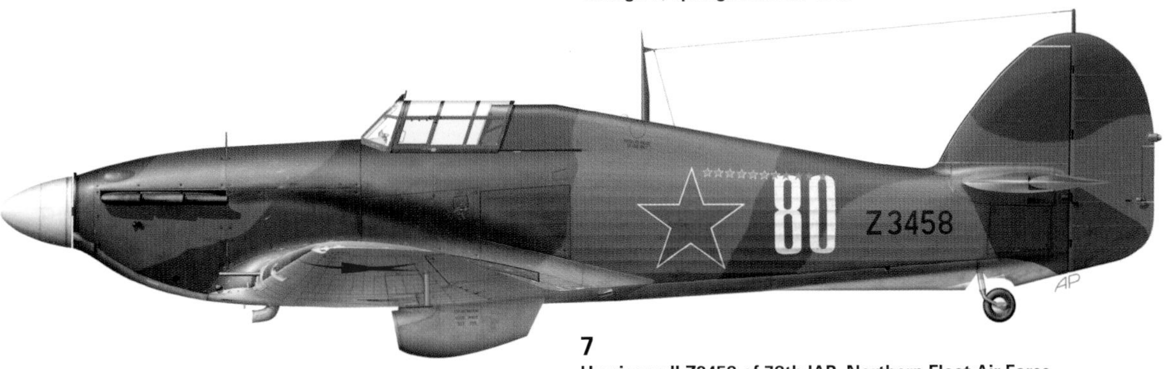

7
Hurricane II Z3458 of 78th IAP, Northern Fleet Air Force, Vaenga-2, June 1943

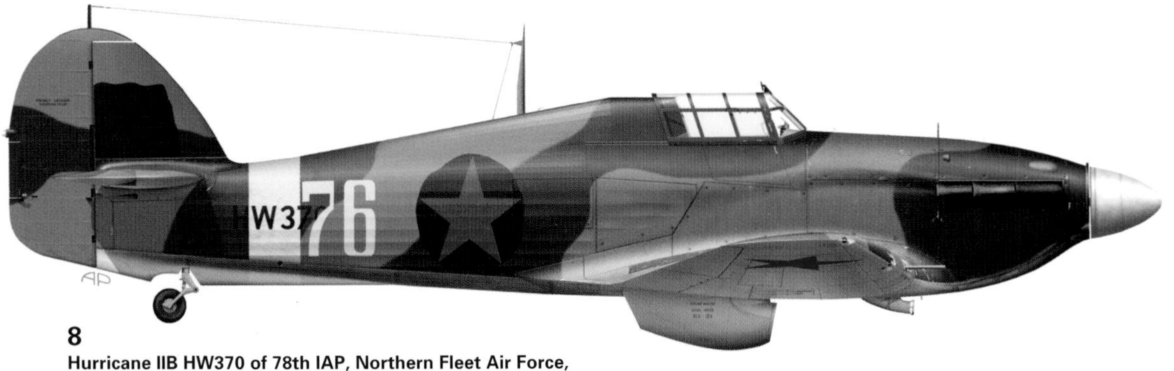

8
Hurricane IIB HW370 of 78th IAP, Northern Fleet Air Force, Vaenga-2, spring 1943

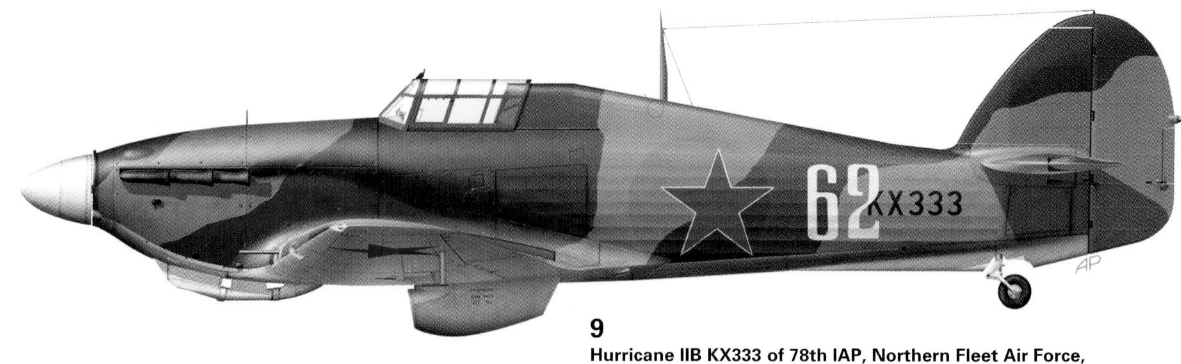

9
Hurricane IIB KX333 of 78th IAP, Northern Fleet Air Force, Vaenga-2, May 1943

10
Hurricane IIB JS280 of 78th IAP, Northern Fleet Air Force, Vaenga-2, 1943

11
Hurricane IIB BD863 of 78th IAP, Northern Fleet Air Force, Vaenga-2, summer 1943

12
Hurricane IIC KX452 of 78th IAP, Northern Fleet Air Force, Vaenga-2, spring 1943

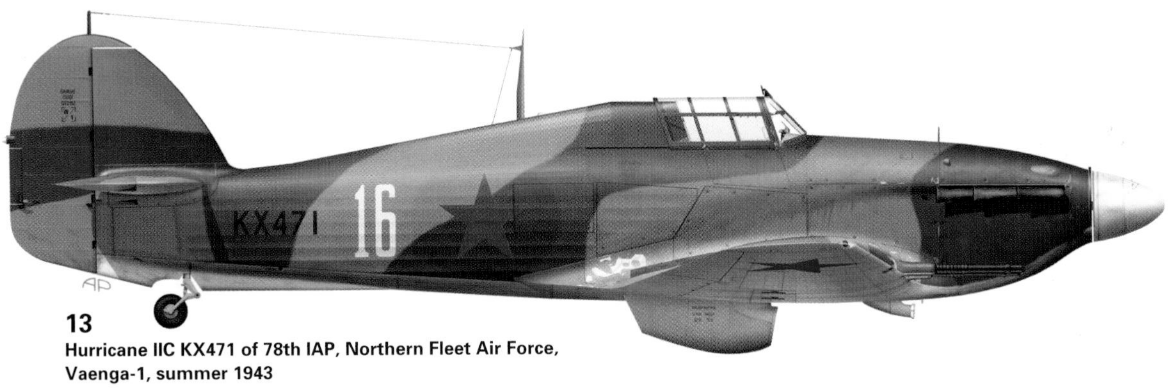

13
Hurricane IIC KX471 of 78th IAP, Northern Fleet Air Force, Vaenga-1, summer 1943

14
Hurricane IIB of 2nd GKAP, Northern Fleet Air Force, Vaenga-2, summer 1942

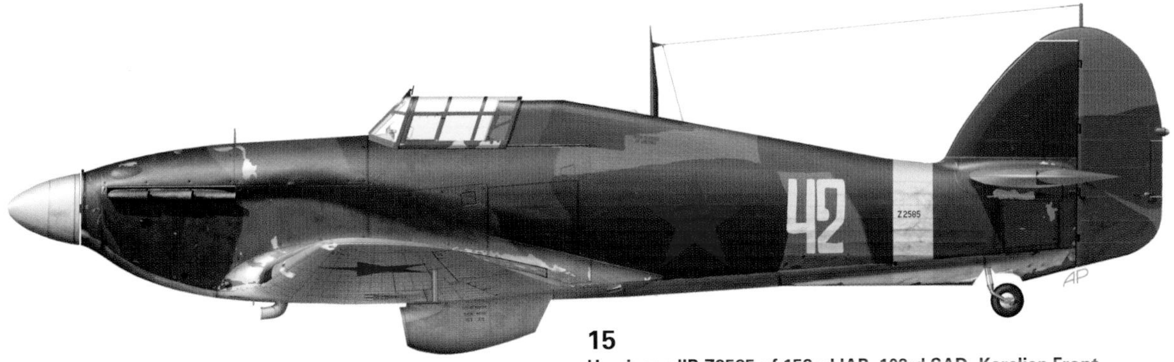

15
Hurricane IIB Z2585 of 152nd IAP, 103rd SAD, Karelian Front Air Force, Boyarskaya, February 1942

16 (port)
Hurricane IIB BM959 of 609th IAP, Karelian Front Air Force, USSR, April 1942

17 (starboard)
Hurricane IIB BM959 of 609th IAP, Karelian Front Air Force, USSR, April 1942

18
Hurricane IIB BH250 of 17th GShAP, Karelian Front Air Force, USSR, summer 1942

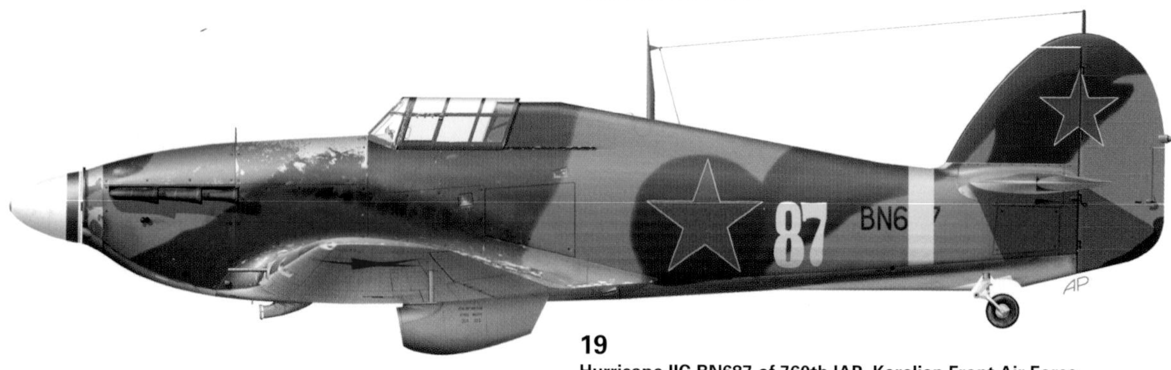

19
Hurricane IIC BN687 of 760th IAP, Karelian Front Air Force, USSR, 1942-43

20
Hurricane IIB Z2751 of 147th IAP, 14th Army Air Force, Murmashi, February 1942

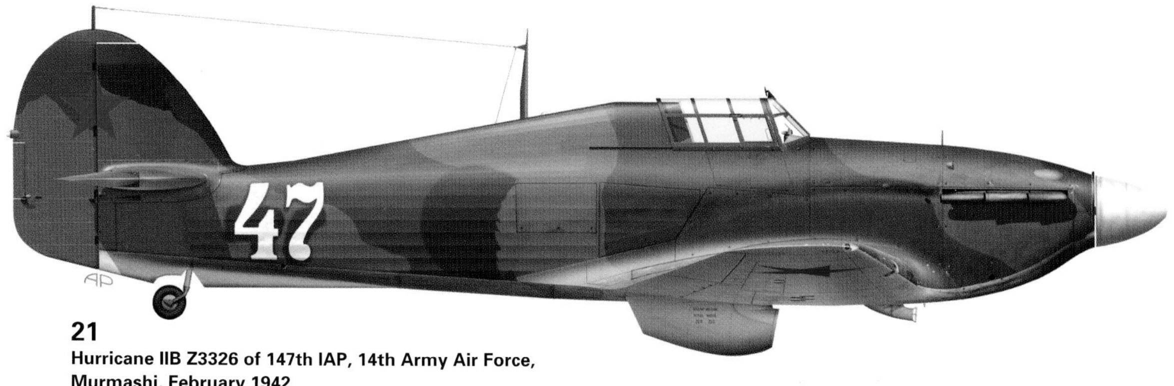

21
Hurricane IIB Z3326 of 147th IAP, 14th Army Air Force, Murmashi, February 1942

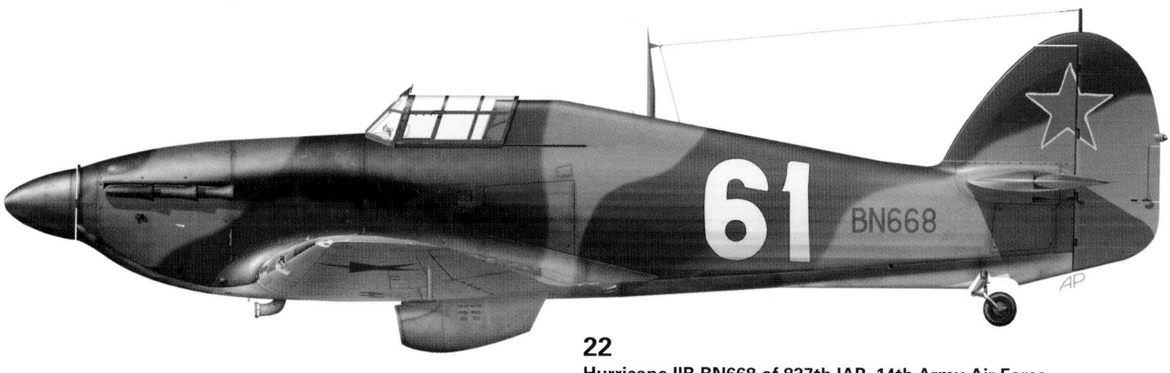

22
Hurricane IIB BN668 of 837th IAP, 14th Army Air Force, Murmashi, September 1942

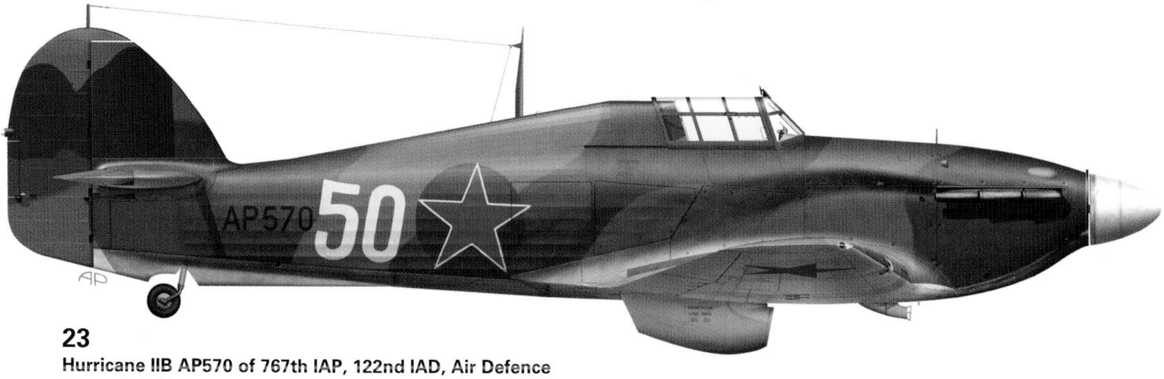

23
Hurricane IIB AP570 of 767th IAP, 122nd IAD, Air Defence Force, Arktika, summer 1942

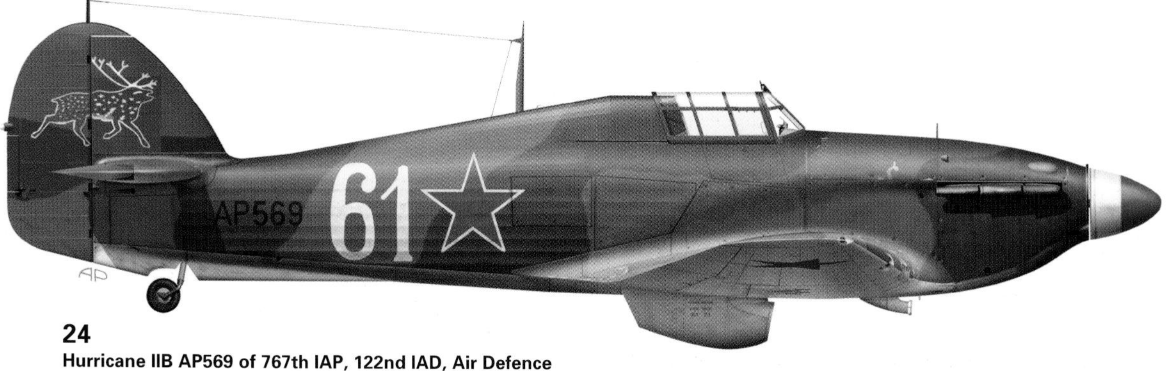

24
Hurricane IIB AP569 of 767th IAP, 122nd IAD, Air Defence Force, Arktika, May 1942

25
Hurricane IIB Z3312 of 767th IAP, 122nd IAD, Air Defence Force, Arktika, May 1942

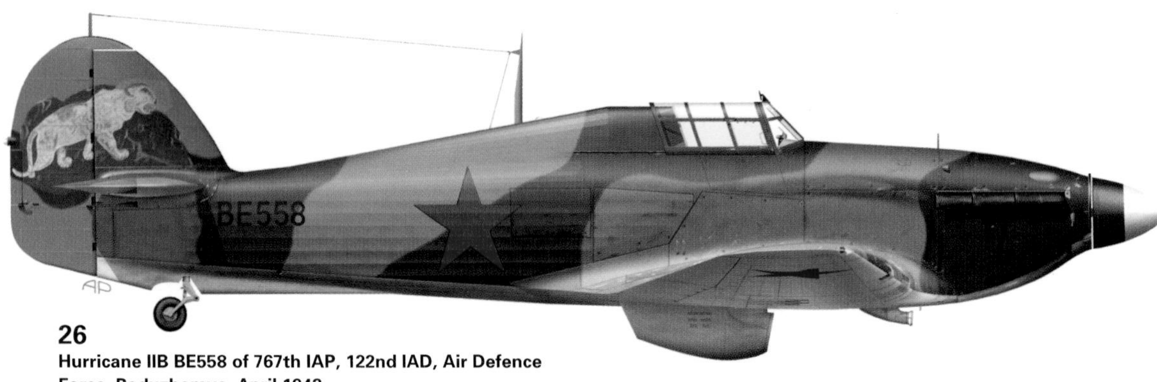

26
Hurricane IIB BE558 of 767th IAP, 122nd IAD, Air Defence Force, Poduzhemye, April 1942

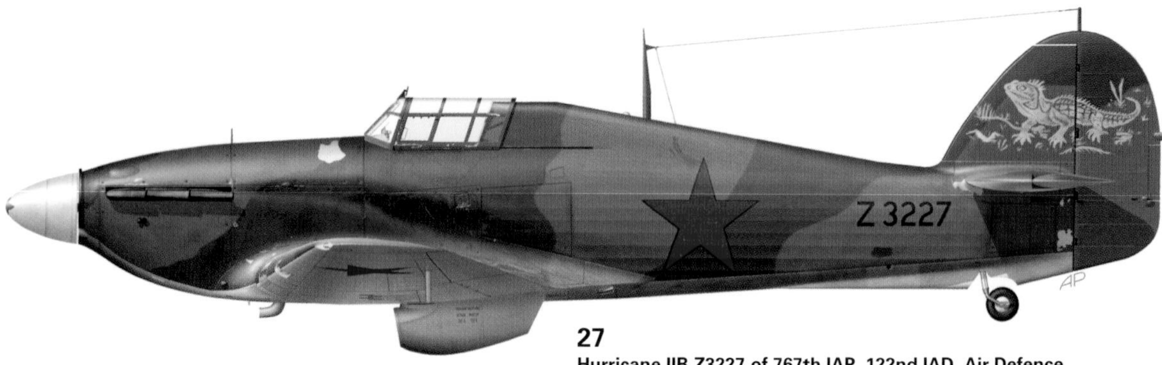

27
Hurricane IIB Z3227 of 767th IAP, 122nd IAD, Air Defence Force, Poduzhemye, March 1942

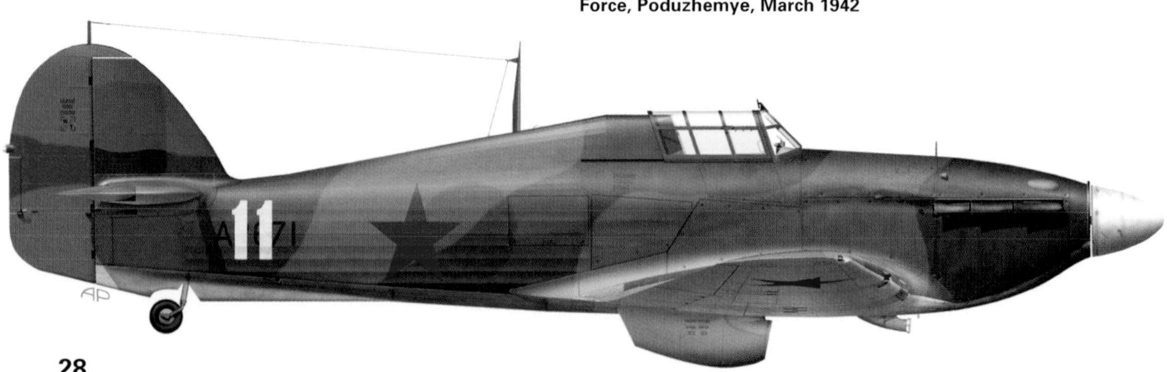

28
Hurricane IIB AP671 of 768th IAP, 122nd IAD, Air Defence Force, Arktika, spring 1942

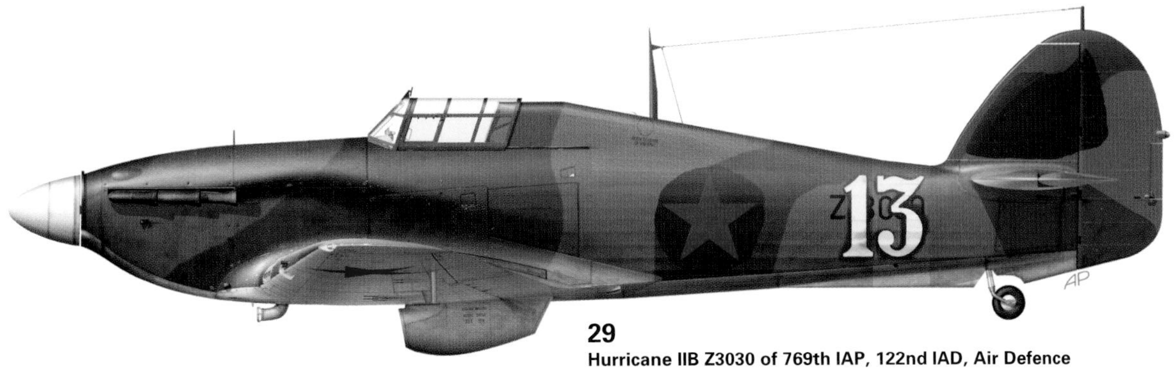

29
Hurricane IIB Z3030 of 769th IAP, 122nd IAD, Air Defence Force, Shonguy, March 1942

30
Hurricane IIB BN416 of 769th IAP, 122nd IAD, Air Defence Force, Poduzhemye, April 1942

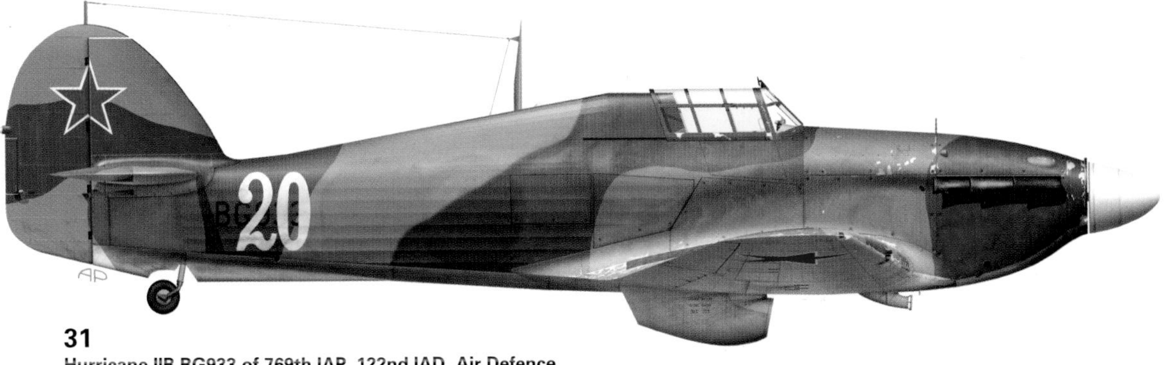

31
Hurricane IIB BG933 of 769th IAP, 122nd IAD, Air Defence Force, Arktika, July 1942

32
Hurricane IIB Z5689 of 730th IAP, 104th IAD, Air Defence Force, Kegostrov, February 1942

In May the regiment received its first four Kittyhawk Is to add to the five surviving Hurricanes that remained on strength. With such a limited number of aircraft available, the regiment engaged in only a handful of missions during the summer months, spending most of its time performing familiarisation and training flights with the new American fighter. There were, however, some engagements with enemy aircraft.

In one of these clashes, on 25 June, Gavrilov provided further proof of his flying skills upon his return to duty following injury. During the early afternoon, notification was received from local air observation, warning and communication posts of the approach of enemy aircraft. Four Brewsters of 3./LeLv 24 had carried out a reconnaissance mission over the Kirov railway line, prompting the 152nd's duty flight of Hurricanes to scramble after them. Two fighters soon returned, but Sgt Repin spotted the enemy aircraft and set off in pursuit. He also notified his base of his discovery, and three Kittyhawk Is (some sources indicate that only two Curtiss fighters were involved) and three more Hurricanes were scrambled. These machines, led by Gavrilov, intercepted the intruders and engaged them in combat.

Minutes later two pairs of Brewsters from 2./LeLv 24 were scrambled under the command of Lauri Okhukaijnen, these machines being vectored to the aerial battle that was being fought between the Kirov railway line and Segozero. When the Finnish reinforcements arrived on the scene there were three separate combats taking place within the main battle, which lasted for about 15 minutes.

The first to break off combat were the Brewsters of 3./LeLv 24, as they were running short of fuel and the battle was raging over Soviet territory. Pilots from 2./LeLv 24 duly followed them minutes later, with

Pilots of 17th GShAP on the Karelian Front are briefed for a mission. On 30 April 1942, while targeting German forces near Segezh, Hurricanes from this regiment shot down Do 17P Wk-Nr. 3547 (1R+CH) of the *F-Kette Lappland* reconnaissance unit. Documents detailing the names of the Soviet pilots involved have not yet come to light

the Soviet pilots in pursuit. It was at this point that the Finnish pilots started to make mistakes. The first to be shot down was Kalervo Ilmari Anttila, wingman of Lauri Ohukainen, who reacted too late to save him. Trailing a plume of black smoke, the damaged Brewster headed west, but the Finnish pilot did not make it back over the frontline. Nevertheless, having landed his damaged aircraft in a marsh, Anttila was able to return to friendly territory suffering nothing more serious than numerous bites from forest midges.

Having lost his wingman, Lt Ohukainen managed to escape from his pursuers, but only for a short time. Flying at an altitude of 100 m (325 ft) over the waters of Segozero lake on full power, his B-239 (BW-372) was, to the pilot's surprise, attacked by a pair of Hurricanes. Its engine was damaged in the first attack and its port side riddled. Thick black smoke immediately began pouring from the aircraft. The starboard side and fuel tank were set on fire in the second attack and the aircraft was engulfed in flames. Ohukainen landed on the water without reducing speed and the Brewster flipped over in the crash. Somehow the Finnish pilot survived the impact with the water and managed to escape from his sinking aircraft (which was recovered from the lake in 1998 and is now on display in the Finnish Air Force Museum). Ohukainen swam to shore, and after a 20 km (16-mile) walk, he was able to reach friendly troops.

The Finnish pilot would later recall in his memoirs that his flight had faced a force of about 15 Hurricanes and MiGs. Moreover, he made a point of noting that the Hurricanes were more manoeuvrable and faster than the Brewsters. Judging by the reports made by pilots of 152nd IAP, it was senior political commissar V N Faerman who had forced the Finnish pilot to take his involuntary dip, Ohukainen being Faerman's third victory with the Hurricane. In all, the Soviet pilots reported the destruction of three Brewsters. The second had been claimed by Snr Lt Gavrilov and Sgt I A Repin, the latter pilot having subsequently been killed in the same action.

The Finns reported that seven Hurricanes had been destroyed, these being claimed as individual kills by pilots of 2./LeLv 24. However, 152nd IAP lost only Repin's Hurricane (Z3096), the sergeant pilot having fought a single-handed battle that went unnoticed by his comrades. According to the Finns, Z3096 started a forest fire after hitting the ground. It is likely that Repin was burned along with the aircraft, and to this day he remains listed as missing without trace.

On 6 August 152nd IAP's two aces, Capt Gavrilov and Snr Lt Basov, came within a hair's breadth of death during a reconnaissance sortie. By then both men had switched to the Kittyhawk I. Having photographed the Finnish airfield of Tiliksjarvi and then attacked it with two FAB-100 bombs, the Soviet pilots had to dodge bursts of flak as they set course for home. They were then bounced from above by five Brewsters of 2./LeLv 24,

On 21 March 1942 Hurricane IIB Z3227 of 767th IAP crash-landed at Poduzhemye airfield after a training flight. The pilot, Jr Lt V I Grigoryev, had allowed his speed to drop too much on approach and the undercarriage and propeller were damaged in the subsequent hard landing

Hastily camouflaged with a handful of branches cut down from nearby trees, a heavily exhaust-stained Hurricane IIB rests between sorties at an undisclosed airfield on the Karelian Front during the summer of 1942

Gavrilov spotting them as they closed from behind. Opening his throttle, he broke away from his pursuers, who focused their attack on Basov. When the latter failed to return to base, it was initially thought that he had perished, as several searches for him revealed nothing. The following note appeared in the regimental diary;

'The regiment has lost one of its best men, one of Stalin's proud falcons, our respected comrade Vladimir Basov.'

But there was good news ten days later. Basov was reported as lying severely wounded in a hospital bed. He later stated that he had shot down two Brewsters – claims not confirmed by Finnish records – during an uneven dogfight. The career of squadron commander Capt Vladimir Basov, however, came to an end at the same time. The wounds he had received fighting the B-239s were so severe that he was unable to return to action. With 240 combat sorties to his name, he had completed more missions than any of his colleagues up to that point in the war. Basov had survived eight dogfights, during which he claimed five individual and one shared victories. He was awarded the order of the Red Banner on 27 October 1942.

Gavrilov, by comparison, had flown 95 operational sorties and survived eight dogfights by the beginning of August. He received his second Order of Lenin for his achievements by order of the commander of the Karelian Front, dated 12 October 1942.

By the end of 1942 only four Hurricanes and three Kittyhawks remained in service with 152nd IAP, and all were defective. The combat report for the month of December noted that 'the regiment did not engage in any military action while based at Segezha airfield because its equipment was not up to full strength, there was a lack of combat activity by ground forces and weather conditions were bad'.

152nd IAP was down to just two Hurricanes and three Kittyhawks by March 1943, and shortly thereafter it was reformed in a three squadron

Wearing full-length leather coats, pilots from 609th IAP of the Karelian Front Air Force await the call to scramble. Note the parachute forward of the cockpit. During the first half of 1942 pilots from this regiment flew Hurricane IIs and LaGG-3s. Although both types were available in equal numbers, the Hurricanes flew more missions due to their better serviceability rates

format as part of 259th IAD and re-deployed to Kandalaksha with a single mission – to protect the local railway line from attacks by Ju 87s of 4./StG 5. The dive-bombers were escorted by the experienced fighter pilots of II./JG 5 *Eismeer*, which was equipped with Bf 109Fs and Gs.

The 'Gustavs' were distinguished by their heavier armament. A pair of 20 mm MG 151 cannon were mounted in underwing pods, these weapons supplementing the standard armament of a MG 151 firing through the propeller hub and a pair of 7.92 mm MG 17 machine guns fitted above the engine. As a result, the new Bf 109G-2/R6 was able to deliver a weight of fire of 5.05 kg (11 lb) per second, which was considerably superior to 152nd IAP's Soviet-modified Hurricanes, which mounted two 20 mm ShVAK cannon and two 12.7 mm UB heavy machine guns that were able to deliver a weight of fire of 3.84 kg (8.5 lb) per second.

With the introduction of the Bf 109G, the advantage in the head-on attacks that started most air battles began to swing towards the Luftwaffe pilots. This left their Soviet counterparts in a difficult position, as the sole tactical advantage they had enjoyed with the Hurricane had been lost. For 152nd IAP a new chapter in the air war had commenced. The German pilots in their Bf 109Gs represented a considerably stronger and more deadly foe than the Finns with their mostly obsolete equipment.

In early March 1943, at its new base at Gremyakha airfield, 152nd IAP received a further 15 Hurricane IICs drawn from other units to supplement their worn-out

The issuing of heavily armed Bf 109G-2/R6s to JG 5 in 1943 further negated the advantage previously enjoyed by Soviet-modified Hurricanes in head-on attacks

survivors. The new arrivals were armed with four 20 mm HS 404 Hispano cannon providing 5.64 kg (12.5 lb) of fire per second, which went some way to improving a Soviet pilot's chances in an encounter with the more modern Bf 109G-2/R6. The new Hurricanes were delivered dismantled and packed in wooden crates to a rear airfield, where the regiment's technical personnel were immediately sent to assemble them. This was to prove a difficult and time-consuming task, as there were no Russian-language manuals supplied with the aircraft. Particular problems were experienced with the guns, which were found to be complex to install and set up.

152nd IAP began combat operations from its new location virtually immediately. The regiment shared Gremyakha with other units that were also equipped with Hurricanes, namely 760th, 768th and 966th air defence IAPs. Each unit was assigned its own sector of the Kirov railway line to defend, and usually they were expected to do so unaided. However, the most dangerous sector, and the one that suffered the most intensive bombardment by enemy bombers, was that assigned to 152nd IAP. Combat reports of the initial clashes indicate that the regiment's pilots acquitted themselves well, with formations of dive-bombers, escorted by just two or three Bf 109s, tending to turn away and jettison their bombs short of the target when encountering Soviet fighter patrols.

These first battles ended without loss to the Soviet pilots, who often returned to report enemy aircraft destroyed. During the morning of 12 March seven Hurricanes of 152nd IAP, led by Gavrilov, encountered a formation of enemy aircraft that the Soviet pilots took to be three Ju 87s and three Bf 109s. However, during the ensuing battle, the 'Ju 87s' unexpectedly raised their undercarriages to reveal themselves as Bf 109s. Yet this rapid transformation from 'dive-bomber' to 'fighter' did not worry the 152nd's pilots unduly, as they had been reinforced by two pairs of Hurricanes from 966th IAP just minutes earlier. As a result of the combined action the Soviet pilots reported shooting down five Bf 109s, three being claimed by 152nd IAP and two by 966th IAP, although none of the claims were confirmed. Gavrilov was credited with two individual and one shared kills.

Subsequent clashes would reveal the strength of the enemy force in this location, and the danger it posed. On 18 March Soviet pilots were ordered to attack Alakurtti airfield and destroy German aircraft there. However, the defences, both flak and fighters, took a heavy toll of the attackers. Of the four Il-2s of 828th Attack Air Regiment (*Shturmovoy Aviatsionniy Polk*, ShAP) taking part, none returned. Two were shot down by flak and two by fighters. All the crew members perished apart from one who was able to return to his unit on foot five days later nursing a head wound.

152nd IAP also suffered. Its pilots had been escorting the Il-2s, and all but one of the five Hurricanes involved were shot down (aircraft numbers 519, 545, BN823 and 938). Only Gavrilov managed to avoid the carnage. He eventually succeeded in shaking off the Messerschmitt that had pursued him almost back to base. Two young pilots, MSgts I S Zagorodnikov and N S Kharlamov, were killed, but Sgt G M Sukhov surviveed after belly landing on a frozen lake and escaping from his machine prior to it being strafed by Bf 109s.

Gavrilov's luck ran out four days later, however. On 22 March he was leading six Hurricanes that had been scrambled to intercept enemy dive-bombers. The Soviet fighters reached their objective just as the Ju 87s pulled off their target and were setting course for home. As they pursued the Stukas, the Hurricanes were in turn attacked from above by two groups of Bf 109s. By making a left-hand turn and forming a defensive circle at an altitude of about 600 m (1950 ft), the Hurricane pilots started to break away from the fighters. Whilst some of the Messerschmitts fired at the Hurricanes from above, others descended to 200 m (650 ft) and attacked from below. As a result of this pincer movement, the German pilots succeeded in destroying three Hurricanes.

The fuel tank of one Hurricane (BN518) exploded in the first attack and the aircraft tumbled out of the sky in a steep dive. The stricken fighter, together with its pilot, squadron commander Snr Lt Ivan Medvedev, penetrated the ice like a hot torch and sank. Another pilot, Snr Lt S A Rogachevskiy, bailed out of his burning aircraft and managed to walk back to his unit, despite having suffered a foot wound.

Fatally injured, Capt Gavrilov made an emergency landing near Zhemchuzhnaya station. By the time he was found beside his Hurricane, Gavrilov was dead. Prior to succumbing to his wounds, the ace had written 'I die for my Motherland' in his own blood on the fuselage of his fighter. Following this battle, Gavrilov and Medvedev were posthumously credited with the shared destruction of a Ju 87.

Without their leader, the remaining 152nd IAP pilots broke off the combat. Snr Lt Pavel Levchuk and Jr Lt Petr Churkin escaped at low level, while Jr Lt Timofey Ryabchenko headed for the clouds, his damaged aircraft leaking hydraulic fluid. As he climbed to safety, Ryabchenko saw six Bf 109s heading west at low level in line astern. After two weeks of active combat 152nd IAP had only two serviceable Hurricanes left.

By the time of his death Pavel Ivanovich Gavrilov was the leading Soviet Air Force Hurricane ace serving on the Karelian Front, having claimed one Fokker D.XII, three B-239s, one Blenheim and two Bf 109s destroyed. Five of these aircraft had been shot down while Gavrilov was flying the Hurricane. He was also credited with sharing in the destruction of two more Bf 109s and a Ju 87.

There were, of course, many other successful Soviet Air Force fighter pilots on the Karelian Front. Some had higher scores than Gavrilov, but none had claimed as many victories while flying Hurricanes. HSU V I Krupskiy of 760th IAP, for example, claimed to have shot down nine enemy aircraft, but he only accounted for one of them as a Hurricane pilot. All of Krupskiy's remaining claims were made while he was flying the Kittyhawk. Of the eight individual kills credited to the other famous Karelian Front ace, HSU Aleksander Nikolaenkov, also of 760th IAP, two were made while he was flying the Hurricane – these were his first and last kills. Sandwiched in between these successes were six victories that he claimed while flying the Kittyhawk I.

No other aces of the Soviet Air Force who fought in the skies over the polar region and Karelia in this most difficult and bloody period of the war achieved the same level of success as Pavel Ivanovich Gavrilov in the Hurricane.

NORTHERN FLEET ACES

It was hardly surprising that the Northern Fleet Air Force should have had within its ranks more Hurricane aces than any other in the Soviet Union during the Great Patriotic War with Germany, as its pilots were engaged in combat operations with the Hawker fighter for nearly two-and-a-half years. As a result 13 Northern Fleet Air Force Hurricane pilots shot down five or more enemy aircraft between September 1941 and January 1944. Among them was Petr Grigoryevich Sgibnev, who recorded 11 kills in 1942 alone to make him the ranking Soviet Air Force Hurricane ace. Up until his death on 3 May 1943, Sgibnev had achieved an overall score of 19 individual victories. He ranks as the second highest scoring ace in the Northern Fleet Air Force, behind only the legendary twice HSU recipient Lt Col Boris Feoktistovich Safonov, who was credited with 20 individual kills.

Boris Safonov was the Northern Fleet Air Force's top-scoring ace. He was also the first of its pilots to destroy an enemy aircraft, performing that feat on 24 June 1941 when he downed Ju 88A Wk-Nr. 8173 while flying an I-16. On 16 September Safonov was awarded the title of HSU and the Order of Lenin. Later he received the Order of the Red Banner three times and the British Distinguished Flying Cross on 19 March 1942. Safonov was killed in aerial combat on 30 May 1942, having achieved a total score of 20 victories. Of his 219 combat missions, 44 were flown in Hurricanes, and his two aerial engagements with the type resulted in two kills – over a Bf 109 on 17 December and an He 111 on 31 December 1941

The first Hurricanes operated by the Northern Fleet Air Force were those handed over by the RAF's No 151 Wing, whose pilots flew alongside the Soviet airmen in Arctic skies for more than two months. On 25 October 1941 these aircraft were issued to newly formed 78th IAP, which was established at Vaenga-1 with three squadrons and commanded by Boris Safonov. The unit's pilots were drawn from 72nd Combined Aviation Regiment (*Smeshannaya Istrebitelniy Aviapolk*, SAP), which had been active during the summer without any great success. Although 72nd SAP pilots had not downed any enemy aircraft whilst flying I-16s during this period, once assigned to 78th IAP they soon used their ex-RAF Hurricanes to claim a Bf 110 destroyed. Its destruction was not officially confirmed, however.

Standing second from left in this group photograph of 2nd GKAP pilots is Snr Lt D I Sinev, who, on 25 October 1941, according to official records, became the first Soviet Hurricane pilot to shoot down an enemy aircraft

Archival sources now available to historians reveal that the majority of victories attributed to Soviet fighter pilots in World War 2 were actually unconfirmed. At most only about a third were verified, which means that out of five or six claimed only two can be regarded as actual kills. In some cases none of the victories attributed to pilots hitherto can be confirmed. Perhaps then it is only fair to devote some space in this volume to those pilots who did not become aces at the time but who nevertheless scored real victories in the early stages of the Hurricane's career in the USSR.

It was almost immediately after 78th IAP had been formed that Northern Fleet fighter pilots filed their first claim. As previously noted, on 25 October 1941 six Hurricanes of the regiment's 1st Squadron, led by Snr Lt V P Rodin, engaged a formation of Bf 110s in a head-on attack over the frontline near Zapadnaya Litsa. Lt D I Sinev fired at one fighter that was subsequently seen emitting smoke and diving sharply towards the ground. Reports from other pilots acted as confirmation of this kill. The German pilots of 1.(Z)/JG 77 claimed to have given 'as good as they got', and Leutnant Feliks-Maria Brandis reported shooting down a Hurricane over the frontline shortly after the initial skirmish. In reality neither side had suffered any losses.

The first Luftwaffe aircraft to definitely fall victim to Northern Fleet Hurricane pilots was Ju 52/3m Wk-Nr. 5974 of *Tr.St.Fl.Fü.Nord.* The aircraft had suffered compass failure and its crew had lost their way, blundering into Soviet-controlled airspace. The lumbering tri-motor transport was intercepted by a flight of Hurricanes near Belokamenki and shot down by Lt V V Kravchenko. The Ju 52/3m's pilot, Feldwebel Rudolf Pesnak, managed to land the burning aircraft on the tundra, but seven men from an airfield construction brigade who were on board were overcome by smoke and died. Another was shot while being captured and the remaining six passengers and crew were taken prisoner.

The Hurricane pilots shot down their first German combat aircraft on 17 December when, on this short and gloomy polar day, five Hurricanes led by Maj Safonov encountered seven Bf 109Es of 14./JG 77 near the frontline. The Soviet pilots engaged the German fighters at an altitude of 2000 m (6500 ft), and exploiting their superior manoeuvrability, they damaged Bf 109E-7 Wk-Nr. 4081 so severely that Leutnant Alfred Jakobi, who had been wounded in the shoulder, was forced to limp back to his airfield, where his aircraft was declared beyond repair.

However, two Hurricanes had also been lost during the clash with the Bf 109s, Lt M G Volkov being killed and Safonov having to make an emergency landing on a frozen lake after his engine stopped with connecting rod failure. A UT-2 search aircraft swiftly located the regimental commander and flew him back to Vaenga-2, leaving his Hurricane to be finished off by German fighters a few days later.

Official records state that four pilots claimed the honour of being

Snr Lt V V Kravchenko of 78th IAP was one of the first Northern Fleet Air Force pilots to shoot down an enemy aircraft while flying a Hurricane. On 16 November 1941 he destroyed a Ju 52/3m to score his third victory of the war. Kravchenko was killed in aerial combat on 10 May 1942 shortly after shooting down his fourth German aircraft

The remains of Ju 52/3m Wk-Nr. 5974 of the *Tr.St.Fl.Fü.Nord,* which was shot down by Snr Lt Kravchenko. The transport aircraft was carrying German military construction workers from Rovaniemi to Kirkenes when its crew lost their bearings due to navigation instrument failure and blundered into Soviet-controlled airspace

the first to down an enemy aircraft while flying a Hurricane on 17 December – Safonov, Capt Markevich, Lt Sinev and the now-deceased Lt Volkov. Today, it is virtually impossible to determine which of the quartet was actually responsible for the only Messerschmitt loss in this battle.

But there is no doubt about the identity of the pilot responsible for the next Hurricane kill. Snr Lt Dmitriy Reutov shot down an He 111 bomber on the last day of 1941 to score his first victory, and the year's tenth for 78th IAP. German sources confirm that He 111H-6 Wk-Nr. 4357 of 1./KG 26 failed to return from a sortie that day.

Three Heinkels had left Banak for Luostari airfield the previous day in preparation for a raid on the port of Murmansk. On 31 December they failed to rendezvous with their escort of Bf 109s from 14./JG 77 near the target, probably because of poor visibility in the area. Accordingly, the bomber crews, who were now relying on the polar gloom for protection, arrived over the target without fighter cover. They bombed from 6000 m (19,500 ft) and then turned west, flying in 'V' formation. Thinking the worst part of their mission was already

Maj Gen A A Kuznetsov, commander of the Northern Fleet Air Force, prepares to take off from Vaenga-1 in ex-No 151 Wing Hurricane IIB V5252 in late October 1941. This Gloster-built aircraft had been issued new to the RAF just weeks prior to it being despatched to the USSR aboard HMS *Argus*

Maj Gen Kuznetsov emerges from the cockpit of V5252 following an orientation flight in October 1941. Being the ranking aviator at Vaenga-1 in the autumn of 1941, Kuznetsov became the first Soviet pilot to fly an RAF Hurricane, followed soon after by Boris Safonov

behind them, the crews relaxed their vigilance. It was only when the dark grey clouds were lit up by tracer rounds that the gunners woke up and returned fire. For one of the Heinkels it was already too late because its left-hand engine was on fire.

Having dealt the bomber a telling blow in his first pass, Reutov repositioned himself for an attack on the He 111's tail. As he closed in the German gunner's weapon jammed, allowing the Soviet pilot to fire at the second engine from close range. That too was set ablaze, forcing the pilot of the bomber to make an emergency landing – the burning aircraft ditched in Lake Kildin, not far from the shore. The crew managed to escape from the sinking aircraft in their inflatable dinghy, but they were unable to evade capture by the Soviets.

By the end of 1941 the Northern Fleet Air Force had 30 Hurricanes distributed evenly between 78th IAP and 72nd SAP, the latter unit being in the process of becoming 2nd Guards Combined Air Regiment of the Red Banner (abbreviated in official documents to 2nd GKAP). One of its squadrons was equipped with aircraft supplied under lend-lease, the unit commander of the Northern Fleet Air Force, Maj Gen A A Kuznetsov, making it clear that he expected his experienced pilots to become familiar with their new equipment in the shortest possible time. The technical personnel were ordered to assemble the Hurricanes by 15 January so that the regiment could be ready for operations by the 20th. According to operational reports from Northern Fleet Air Force headquarters, 2nd GKAP's pilots flew their first Hurricane sortie on 29 January, when nine fighters took off to patrol overhead the Northern Fleet's main base.

During the 1942 spring campaign that followed it was 78th IAP and 2nd GKAP that bore the brunt of the fighting against the Luftwaffe on the Kola Peninsula. An indication of the high cost both units paid during the course of these battles is the fact that to maintain their strength during the first half of the year, the Northern Fleet Air Force received 80 Hurricanes in all, not counting those handed over by No 151 Wing upon its departure in late October 1941.

Hurricanes from 78th IAP fly in close formation with an SB bomber during one of the unit's first escort missions in late 1941. Despite the freezing temperatures, the pilots all appear to be flying with the their canopies open!

The son of a factory worker living in Omsk, Sergey Kurzenkov was born in 1911. After graduation from the Textile Technical School, he worked in a textile factory and also learnt to fly at his local aeroclub. In 1933 he entered Eysk Naval Aviation School, and when the war commenced he was serving as an instructor at the Nikolaev Naval Aviation School. In October 1941 Kurzenkov was posted to 78th IAP of the Northern Fleet Air Force, and he scored his first aerial victory on 4 March 1942 while flying a Hurricane. By the time Kurzenkov was shot down in error by Soviet anti-aircraft fire on 23 February 1943 he had increased his tally to eight kills, all in the Hurricane. Seriously wounded in the incident, Kurzenkov could not return to frontline flying. Forced to continue his service as a staff officer, he was awarded the title of HSU on 23 July 1943. He also received the Order of the Red Banner twice, as well as the US Navy Cross

So it was that the combat careers of many Northern Fleet Air Force pilots began during the polar winter, a time when darkness lifted for only a few hours. These men would later be distinguished by the combat successes they achieved in the Arctic theatre of operations. Two pilots stand head and shoulders above the others during this period, Pavel Orlov and Sergey Kurzenkov.

Both arrived in the far north in October 1941 and both held the rank of senior lieutenant. They had been posted to the frontline from a flying school where they had been instructors and flight commanders, although they were mere 'rank and file' pilots when they reported for duty at an operational regiment. However, the advanced flying training they had undergone when being taught how to instruct quickly became apparent, and both pilots soon stood out from their regimental colleagues in terms of their combat success. Orlov and Kurzenkov served in 78th IAP, but in different squadrons, and there was constant friendly rivalry between them. If one had shot down an enemy aircraft, the other would usually claim a kill just a few hours later. Yet their military careers had not begun in the same way.

Sergey Kurzenkov's career as a fighter pilot might have been over almost before it started. On one of his first sorties, while leading a flight patrolling overhead its Vaenga-2 base at night, Kurzenkov mistakenly attacked a friendly Pe-2. The Soviet twin-engined bomber had a silhouette similar to the German Bf 110 heavy fighter. Luckily for them, the crew of the damaged bomber managed to make an emergency belly landing on their own airfield. A few days after it was repaired, the Pe-2 was shot down by enemy fighters and its entire crew perished. Kurzenkov was arrested following the night engagement, and it was only thanks to the intercession of Maj Safonov that he remained in the unit.

But fate had certainly not done with Sergey Kurzenkov, for he was almost shot down during his first encounter with enemy fighters. Later, in his memoirs, Kurzenkov would recall that dogfight on 4 January 1942;

'The Henschel 126 observation aircraft would cross the frontline almost every day and fly over the mountains close to the forward positions of our land forces. The Fascists found something there because they immediately reported the coordinates back to their own artillery batteries. The barrage would begin and the Henschels would cruise around to correct the fire. The soldiers had become really tired of the "Sticks", as they were known on account of their ugly appearance, but they weren't able to shoot them down – the Henschels were heavily armoured.

'We were in turn given the job of hunting down the Henschels, but they were nowhere to be seen. We would fly to the frontline and still see nothing – they'd been warned by German observation posts on the mountain peaks and disappeared. The mountains would slide by under our wings once again and the gorges would darken, but still there was no sign of the Henschels. There was no trace of them

'Our flight took off again in pursuit of Henschels on 4 January, but once more without success. We flew along the frontline for about an hour before turning for home empty handed. I was the last in a line of three Hurricanes, and for me at the back it was like a shuttle flight. I started to make some shallow turns to the left and the right. I made the next turn to the right over the coastal cliffs of the Gulf of Ura-Gubsky and suddenly I felt a strange sensation. I looked back just in time to see some "Messers" chasing us, trailing black smoke, and now they'd caught up with us. One began an attack from behind and to the right. "I'll take him head-on!" I thought to myself. I managed to shout a warning to my colleagues over the radio as I threw the aircraft into a half-roll. The Fascists opened fire. The tracers rushed towards me in a colourful volley. "Don't turn away! Don't turn away!", I told myself, pressing my face against the gunsight.

'I pressed the firing button several times but none of the rockets – RS-82 Katyushas – flew out from under the wings. Then I pressed the trigger for the machine guns. A shower of tracer bullets spewed from the 12 barrels. The aircraft shook violently, but I didn't take my finger off the trigger until the slender dirty-grey fuselage and stumpy wings of the lead "Messer" had flashed across my gunsight. After a steep turn the Fascist sheltered behind the mountains. A trace of black smoke hung

This map shows airfields (marked with a circled T symbol) that were home to Hurricane regiments defending Murmansk and Kandalaksha in 1941-43

in the air. I let go of the trigger and the guns stopped. A pair of "Messers" flashed past close by and to the left. Throwing a glance over to the right, I saw another two Messerschmitts – the covering pair.

'A shiver went down my spine. I dared not look to the right for that would be the end of me. I plunged into a second head-on attack but the "Messers" didn't rise to it. They split up, making combat turns, one to the left, the other to the right. I again felt uncomfortable during this manoeuvre and immediately looked behind. Sure enough, a "Messer" from the first pair was closing on my tail, its yellow nose getting threateningly close. Having sensed danger before actually recognising it, I threw my aircraft into such a steep turn that I nearly hit the cliffs below. This crazy manoeuvre saved me from death, but it didn't save the aircraft. The starboard wing received a long burst of machine gun fire, which violently shook the aircraft and left the wing riddled with ragged holes. There was also a sharp pain in my right thigh.

'Sheltering behind the mountains, I could breathe a little, and had a chance to assess the situation. It was not in my favour. I couldn't see my comrades, nor hear anything on the radio. I was alone against four hostile fighters. The respite lasted just a few seconds, then it began again. Forming a circle above me, four Messerschmitts started to dive, one after the other. And they didn't seem to be worried about wasting ammunition. I only just managed to escape. I took cover behind the mountains and rolled around them like a spinning top. I plunged into the gorges at breakneck speed, the wings almost catching on the cliffs. The Fascists, though, didn't stop firing – it was as if they had an endless supply of ammunition.

'The first few minutes of the uneven battle were torrid, but I gradually calmed down and was able to see better. I even decided on a counter-attack. Its engine howling, my fighter had sat on the tail of a "Messer" several times. Now I trained my sights on the predatory silhouette with its black crosses. I pressed the trigger but the guns were silent. All 12 were out of action, and it was likely that the pneumatic firing mechanism was faulty. I was unarmed. The Fascists probably guessed why I wasn't shooting and insolently stepped up their attacks. Then I remembered the rockets – why hadn't they worked? Seizing the moment, I quickly looked to the left side of my cockpit where there was a small box with a rotating switch in the centre. Sure enough, the switch had spun round. I quickly re-set it and the "Katyushi" were ready for action. I hadn't relied on them in air combat before, but now there was no choice.

'One of the "Messers" was diving towards me. The pilot opened fire. I went behind the mountains. Cannon shells and bullets spattered from every direction, crumbling the granite cliff. I managed to launch a rocket but it exploded just ahead of me, and the Fascist fighter tore away to the side. I fired all my rockets but not one of them caused any damage. In a quick glance at the instrument panel I noticed I was running out of fuel. In another 10 or 15 minutes I would fall out of the sky. I continued to dodge my attackers, and now I started leading them east towards the artillery batteries covering our naval base. Suddenly, I saw six of our fighters flying over the mountains at maximum speed. The '109 pilots also saw them – the Fascists didn't like a dogfight in which we outnumbered them. They broke off their attack and headed west.

These pilots from 78th IAP have gathered for a political meeting at Vaenga-2 airfield during early 1942. They are, from left to right, squadron adjutant Capt I I Belov (back row), Sgt G G Ivanov, unknown sailor, Snr Lt V V Kravchenko, Snr Sgt P D Romanov (front row), Lt S I Verkhovksiy, Lt L L Khrustal, Jr Lt I S Krivoruchko, battalion commissar L A Fedorov (standing) and Snr Lt D I Sinev

'I landed with great difficulty. My hydraulic system had been badly damaged, so when the undercarriage stuck half way down I had to lower the wheels manually. The flaps wouldn't operate either. In the end I couldn't stop the aircraft landing in the middle of the airfield on two wheels. My fighter, its tail raised and with no reduction in speed, was careering towards the edge of the airfield, where huge boulders were looming. The brakes weren't working and I pressed the rudder pedal hard with my left foot. I was trying to avoid the boulders and hoping that the undercarriage would collapse and dump the aircraft on its belly to stop the landing roll, but it drifted like a weathercock in the wind. The tail didn't go down and the aircraft rolled across almost the whole airfield before it stopped. I wanted to jump out of the cockpit but I couldn't. I felt dizzy. Half-an-hour later I was lying on the operating table in our aviation hospital.'

This colourful account suggests that the author not only recalled the details of his encounter with the Messerschmitts but also all of the feelings associated with it. Yet, interesting as such veterans' memoirs are, they are often in conflict with reality. The number of opponents in air combat is usually exaggerated by both sides, and in this case only three Bf 109s were involved. It is also clear that Kurzenkov and his colleagues were not keeping a proper lookout for hostile aircraft because the enemy fighters had been allowed to approach them unseen. As a result they were taken by surprise, and only Kurzenkov survived the encounter to return to base.

The circumstances surrounding the death of Lt P A Krasavtsev remain unknown to this day, although it is possible that he was shot down in one of the Messerschmitts' first surprise attacks. Despite his wounds, Sgt N G Bokiy managed to make an emergency landing in his damaged aircraft on the frontline airfield at Ura-Guba, after which he returned to base on foot. Nikolai Bokiy claimed to have shot down an enemy aircraft prior to his demise, but in reality the Germans had suffered no losses. The Northern Fleet pilots had encountered aircraft of 14./JG 77 flown by Leutnant Alfred Jakobi and Unteroffiziers Dietrich Weinitschke and Artur Mendi. According to Luftwaffe reports, Jakobi and Weinitschke both claimed to have shot down a Hurricane – it was the former's

This Hs 126 artillery spotting aircraft fell victim to a Soviet Hurricane over the frontline in the Murmansk area during the winter of 1941-42

eighth victory. Weinitschke devoted only a few lines of his memoirs to this episode, which he clearly regarded as a routine engagement;

'On that day we engaged seven Hurricanes in combat. Leutnant Jakobi managed to put some holes in one of them, but he sneaked away behind the frontline. Nevertheless, I found him and shot him down. Since Jakobi had taken the first shots at him, he was credited with this victory. I shot down another aircraft beyond the frontline for my third victory, which was confirmed by our ground forces.'

Snr Lt Kurzenkov spent three weeks recovering in hospital.

Enemy reconnaissance aircraft continued to appear regularly over the frontline until finally, on 12 September, two pairs of 78th IAP Hurricanes were scrambled and Snr Lt Pavel Orlov was able to get close enough to a Henschel to open fire from above and behind from a distance of 100-50 m (110-55 yrd). The 'Stick' dived into the ground, its demise watched by jubilant Soviet artillerymen. This Hs 126 was Pavel Orlov's first aerial victory, and he would go on to become one of the most successful Northern Fleet Air Force aces. His victim was Hs 126B Wk-Nr. 4262 of *Kette Petsamo's* 1.(H)/32. Pilot Leutnant Rudolf Krauss and observer Oberfeldwebel Erich Romels were both wounded.

Kurzenkov had scored his first victory six months earlier on 4 March, soon after being discharged from hospital. That day 78th IAP launched a major operation against the Luftwaffe airfield at Luostari, near Murmansk. The Hurricanes attacked in two waves, and the second was intercepted by Bf 109s over the airfield.

Upon returning to base, the Hurricane pilots reported that worthwhile results had been achieved during strafing runs on Luostari airfield. They claimed that a Bf 109, a Ju 88 and an He 111 had been destroyed, together with 15 vehicles. Up to 25 soldiers were also said to have been killed. No fewer than five Bf 109s were allegedly shot down (these remained unconfirmed) and seven damaged in the air and on the ground, along with ten vehicles. However, according to the Central Naval Archive, two flights of Pe-2 photo-reconnaissance aircraft failed to provide photographic evidence of 78th IAP's success. According to German accounts, three He 111s (Wk-Nrs. 4295, 4321 and 4908) of 1./KG 26 were damaged on the ground and written off. This success had come at some cost as the Soviets lost five Hurricanes, although all the

This crude diagram shows how Snr Lt Sergey Kurzenkov despatched a Bf 109 on 4 March 1942

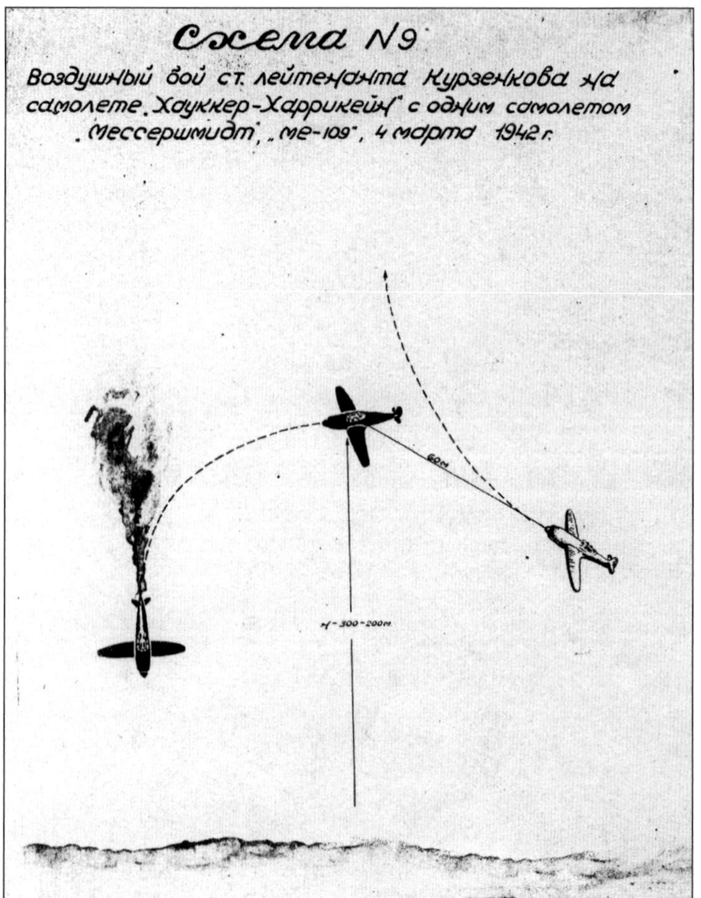

pilots involved survived and managed to evade capture. The Central Naval Archive report of the raid noted;

'Following an attack on airfield targets, Snr Lt Kurzenkov was preparing to rejoin his group and return to his airfield. At that moment he noticed a single Me 109 passing in front of him at an altitude of 200-300 m [650-975 ft]. Kurzenkov immediately decided to attack this aircraft. Having increased the speed of his Hurricane, he closed to within 60 m [65 yrd] of the enemy aircraft, taking up an attacking position above and to the rear. From this position, Kurzenkov fired two bursts of machine gun fire at the Me 109. His fire proved to be accurate and the enemy aircraft dived towards the ground. The attack was so unexpected that the enemy did not even attempt to escape. Snr Lt Kurzenkov's accuracy and decisiveness led to his victory in air combat.'

REORGANISATION

At the end of March 1942 all the surviving Hurricanes, together with technical personnel, from 78th IAP were transferred to 2nd GKAP (formerly 72nd SAP, which had been redesignated as a Guards unit in recognition of the success it had achieved during 1941). At the same time new I-16 and Hurricane-equipped squadrons, with their personnel, were transferred into 78th IAP to restore it to full strength.

Many of the pilots posted into 2nd GKAP had only recently finished their fighter training, and therefore lacked the experience to justify their presence in a unit awarded the coveted Guards title. In an attempt to correct this ambiguity, 2nd GKAP was, by decree of the Northern Fleet Air Force dated 23 March, to be commanded by Maj Boris Safonov, formerly CO of 78th IAP. All three Hurricane squadrons from the regiment went with him. Maj Ivan Tumanov, who had previously commanded 72nd SAP and, briefly, 2nd GKAP, was appointed CO of 78th IAP. In this way all the experienced fighter pilots were transferred to the newly renamed Guards regiment, leaving 78th IAP with the novice aviators. In other changes one new Hurricane squadron was formed and Snr Lt Sgibnev was appointed to command it. He was just 20 years old.

Already a combat veteran, Petr Sgibnev had arrived in the far north in February 1942. From the first days of the war until October 1941 he had fought as a member of the Red Banner Baltic Fleet Air Force, completing 186 combat sorties, participating in 14 aerial battles and shooting down four aircraft during this period. On 13 August 1941 he was awarded the Order of the Red Banner for his combat success. But Sgibnev was twice wounded, and following hospital treatment he was posted to the polar theatre.

In the Northern Fleet Air Force he quickly became familiar with the Hurricane, and on 3 April 1942 he

The leading Soviet Hurricane ace with 11 victories, Petr Sgibnev was born in 1920 to the family of a clerk living in the Tver region. In 1937 he entered Eysk Naval Aviation School and began his military service with a detached squadron of the Baltic Fleet Air Force in August 1940. During the first months of the war Sgibnev managed to score four aerial victories flying I-153 fighters. In February 1942, after recovering from wounds inflicted in combat, Sgibnev was transferred to 78th IAP of the Northern Fleet Air Force. He scored his first Hurricane kill on 3 April 1942, and two months later he was made a squadron commander. In January 1943 he was promoted to CO of the famous 2nd GKAP. Sgibnev was awarded the title of HSU, the Order of the Red Banner three times and the DFC. He was killed in a flying accident on 3 May 1943

Five-victory Hurricane ace Vasiliy Shalaev was born in 1917 in the Kalinin region. In 1937 he entered Eysk Naval Aviation School and began his military service in 1940 with the Baltic Fleet Air Force. In February 1942 Shalaev was transferred to 78th IAP of the Northern Fleet Air Force, and he scored his first aerial victory while flying a Hurricane on 4 April that same year. Twice awarded the Order of the Red Banner, Shalaev was killed on 17 June 1944 when his Po-2 crashed

was able to shoot down his first enemy aircraft in the theatre. Sgibnev's victim was a Bf 109 that had been involved in an attack on Murmansk. German records confirm that Luftwaffe aircraft engaged those of the Northern Fleet Air Force's 122nd IAD, and admit the loss of Bf 109E Wk-Nr. 3523. Another 78th IAP pilot was credited with his first victory that day too, and he would also subsequently become a Hurricane ace. Snr Lt Vasiliy Shalaev claimed to have shot down a Bf 110, although this was not confirmed.

Combat activity in the polar skies became much more intense as March 1942 drew to a close. This was due to an increased effort by the Luftwaffe to disrupt Allied convoys bringing vital supplies to the USSR. Convoy PQ-13 was one of the first to experience a combined attack by submarines and aircraft of the Luftwaffe's 5th Air Fleet, which resulted in five of the 19 vessels that had set out from Reykjavik on 20 March being sunk. At the same time, the port of Murmansk began to suffer systematic mass bombing raids by Ju 87 dive-bombers from I./StG 5 and Ju 88s of KG 30, escorted by Bf 110 and Bf 109 fighters.

There was another factor that defined the violent nature of the air war over the coastal regions of the Arctic Ocean in 1942. Luftwaffe units were reinforced with the arrival of the newly formed JG 5 *Eismeer* at the beginning of the year. At the same time Bf 109F-4s were making their appearance. Until then the Luftwaffe had maintained a limited fighter force in the Murmansk area, with just two units – 1. and 14./JG 77 – operating single-engined fighters in the form of Bf 109E-4s and E-7s throughout 1941. With the arrival of Bf 109F-4s in *geschwader* strength, the Northern Fleet Air Force began suffering heavy losses in combat.

For example, during the last week of April 1942 2nd GKAP lost seven Hurricanes to German fighters. A further four aircraft sustained severe damage, and repairing them proved to be problematic due to a chronic shortage of spare parts for the foreign-made fighters. This in turn meant that they were out of action for long periods. Northern Fleet Air Force losses were especially high on 10 May, when no fewer than ten Hurricanes failed to return from operational sorties and five experienced aviators perished. Yet the Northern Fleet pilots managed to exact retribution during these bloody bouts of air combat. The top-scorers during April and May were Petr Sgibnev with seven victories, Pavel Orlov with six kills and Sergey Kurzenkov with five.

Other Northern Fleet pilots claimed their first successes during this period to set them on their way to becoming Hurricane aces in 1942. They were Snr Lts Konstantin Babiy and Vasiliy Doroshin of 78th IAP, with three kills each, and Snr Lt Aleksey Dizhevskiy and Lt Vasiliy Shalaev, also from 78th IAP, who claimed two apiece. Guards Lt Vasiliy Pronchenko of 2nd GKAP opened his score on 30 May.

Another pilot to achieve success during this period was Aleksander Kovalenko also of 2nd GKAP. He was already an ace by early 1942, having shot down

Pictured here are some of 78th IAP's most successful pilots during the fierce battles with the Luftwaffe over Murmansk in the spring and early summer of 1942. They are, from left to right, Lt Vasiliy Shalaev, Snr Lt Petr Sgibnev, unknown and Snr Lt Konstantin Babiy

Left
The oldest Soviet Hurricane ace, Aleksander Kovalenko was born in 1909 in Kiev, Ukraine. In June 1932 he entered Kacha 1st Military Aviation School, and in December of the following year he began his military service with a ground attack squadron, before serving as a flying instructor. In September 1939 Kovalenko participated in the Soviet-Polish campaign, and several months later, during the Soviet-Finnish 'Winter War', he was posted to the Northern Fleet Air Force. By the time Germany invaded the USSR in June 1941, he was a deputy squadron commander with 72nd SAP, flying I-15bis. On 29 June Kovalenko was wounded by bomb splinters during a Luftwaffe raid on the airfield. He had recovered from his injuries by August, and was subsequently credited with shooting down seven enemy aircraft while flying the I-16. His first Hurricane kill was achieved on 24 March 1942, by which point he was serving with 2nd GKAP. Troubled by health issues caused by his shrapnel wound from June 1941, Kovalenko was forced to prematurely end his flying career in early 1943, by which point his score had reached 14 victories. Transferred to the Eysk Naval Aviation School, Kovalenko was awarded the title of HSU, the Order of the Red Banner twice and the RAF's DFC

seven enemy aircraft while flying I-16 fighters over the Murmansk area in the first six months of the war. Kovalenko subsequently became one of the first Northern Fleet Air Force Hurricane pilots to claim five kills, two of these coming on 15 April when he reported shooting down two Ju 87s during a Luftwaffe raid on the port of Murmansk.

He was not the only one to distinguish himself that day, as his comrades claimed a combined total of 15 enemy aircraft destroyed. None were confirmed, however. The port of Murmansk was attacked twice on the 15th by Ju 87s of I./StG 5, escorted by Bf 110s of 10.(Z)/JG 5 and Bf 109E/Fs of II./JG 5. The 5712-ton British transport vessel *Lancaster Castle* was sunk by the Stukas during the attacks, the vessel suffering a direct hit to its engine room. A railway crane, a drydock and a warehouse were also destroyed in the port itself, while the canteen building caught fire and three railway tracks were severed. A 500 kg bomb fell into a bomb shelter, and although it failed to explode, the building collapsed, killing 21 and injuring eight.

The first raid came at 1405 hrs, and it met negligible opposition – Luftwaffe fighters brushed aside the handful of I-16s and I-153s without difficulty. The second raid, at 1830 hrs, met stiffer opposition, with ten Hurricanes and three MiG-3s of 2nd GKAP being scrambled to intercept the raiders. Leading the defenders was Guards Capt Kovalenko, whose formation was accompanied by nine 78th IAP Hurricanes led by Snr Lt Sgibnev, as well as by a flight of I-153s from 27th IAP. Six Hurricanes of 122nd IAD's 769th IAP also joined in.

Sixteen Stukas, flying in pairs and with a close escort of Bf 110s, approached the target from a height of 3500 m (11,500 ft). Behind them, spaced at intervals of 500-1000 m (1625-3250 ft) and some 500 m higher, came nine Bf 109s. The dive-bombers wheeled around in a 90-degree turn before diving steeply out of the sun one after another. They were accompanied down to 200 m by their close escort, while the Bf 109s kept their distance.

The Guards pilots took off in line astern after receiving word of the approaching German formation, with Capt Kovalenko in front. He was ordered to head to Murmansk at a height of 3500 m (11,375 ft).

Proudly wearing their decorations, Aleksander Kovalenko and Boris Safonov (the top-scoring aces of the Northern Fleet Air Force on the polar front) pose for the camera in the spring of 1942. Their friendship had began during their time as students at Kacha Military Aviation School

This Hurricane IIB from the Northern Fleet Air Force has been fitted with two ShVAK 20 mm cannon and two UB 12.7 mm machine guns

There were only three aircraft in the circuit at that time, and without waiting for the others to join up, Kovalenko led them towards the threatened city. While flying at an altitude of 2500 m (8125 ft) he sighted the enemy aircraft above him, but he considered an attack with just three fighters into the sun unfeasible. Kovalenko duly manoeuvred his small force in behind the bombers while the rest of the Hurricanes and MiG-3s joined him.

As the Stukas commenced their diving attack the Hurricane pilots fired a salvo of rockets into the middle of the enemy formation from a range of 400 m, before splitting up and making individual attacks. Kovalenko opened fire from a range of 200 m, and he continued to fire until he was just ten metres behind his target. He was later to report 'the Ju 87 turned over and the cockpit canopy flew off'. Kovalenko did not have time to see his victim hit the ground as he was attacking a second enemy bomber. Opening fire at 100 m, he watched the Stuka roll over onto its back and tumble earthwards. Again he was too busy to witness its final demise as by then the Bf 109s had arrived on the scene.

Upon their return to base Orlov and Kurzenkov also claimed to have destroyed a Ju 87 apiece, the former reporting;

'At an altitude of 1500 m [5000 ft] and from a range of 250-270 m I opened fire on the Ju 87's engine from behind. The engine was engulfed in smoke and I unleashed a second salvo from above and behind while inverted as the Ju 87 was pulling out of its dive. The aircraft caught fire and there were two tongues of flame coming out of each side of the fuselage. I then gave the dive-bomber another burst. It slowed and went down.'

Orlov overshot the Ju 87, and after making a tight banking turn and scanning the sky, he was unable to locate his adversary. Kurzenkov's report was even briefer;

'I attacked one Ju 87 when it was pulling out of its dive, opening fire from a range of 100 m. After the third burst of machine gun fire the Ju 87 crashed 5-8 km [3-5 miles] west of Murmansk'. For both Soviet pilots these victories represented their fourth in aerial combat.

Most of 78th IAP's Hurricanes, led by Snr Lt Sgibnev, engaged the escorting fighters, thus giving the Guards pilots their chance to attack the Stukas without interference. Sgibnev and his formation waded into the Bf 110s as they pulled out of their dives, the leading group firing three long bursts into the first twin-engined fighter in a head-on attack. According to Sgibnev's report, the Bf 110 'dived steeply and crashed into the ground, leaving a trail of black smoke behind it'.

High-scoring Hurricane ace Pavel Orlov was born in 1914 to a peasant family in the village of Solntsevo, near Moscow. In 1933 he entered Eysk Naval Aviation School and after graduation became an instructor there and, in January 1939, at the Nikolaev Naval Aviation School. He was posted to the Northern Fleet Air Force in 1941 and achieved his first victory on 12 January 1942 while flying a Hurricane. Orlov twice received the Order of the Red Banner (the medals worn above the left breast pocket of his tunic) and he was posthumously awarded the title of HSU after he was killed in aerial combat on 15 March 1943

Sgibnev then attacked a single Bf 109 from behind and slightly below from a range of 150-180 m. He again fired three long bursts, but could not prevent the enemy fighter from breaking off combat and diving away to the west. Sgibnev did not see the Messerschmitt crash so after the battle he claimed just the Bf 110 destroyed. It was his second victory as a Hurricane pilot. Although his own aircraft had been damaged by bullets and shrapnel, it was soon repaired. Two of Sgibnev's squadronmates, Snr Lt Zhivotovskiy and Lt Babiy, both claimed to have downed a Bf 110.

For their part the pilots of the escorting Bf 110s claimed to have destroyed two Hurricanes and a MiG-3. They had stayed above the clouds ready to pounce on lone Soviet aircraft, but they only succeeded in damaging a MiG-3, whose pilot was able to make an emergency

This Bf 110 was assigned to 13.(Z)/JG 5 *Eismeer*. In the spring of 1942 Northern Fleet Air Force Hurricane pilots suffered heavy losses to this unit when they attempted to shoot down these heavily armed fighters in head-on attacks

landing. Neither side had suffered unsustainable losses in the battle over Murmansk.

Orlov and Kurzenkov both achieved their fifth victories on 29 April. At 0447hrs the latter was one of four Hurricane pilots who took off to patrol the frontline following fierce fighting on the ground. At 0530 hrs the Soviet fighters encountered three Bf 110s and four Bf 109s, the four Hurricane pilots attacking the twin-engined fighters head-on in line-abreast formation. Kurzenkov launched four rockets from a range of 1000 m and then opened fire with machine guns from 400 m. According to eyewitness reports from fellow pilots, his victim crashed near the frontline. Guards Snr Lt Amosov and Guards Sgt Cheprunov also shot down a Bf 110 in the head-on attack. German sources, however, state that two Bf 110s of 10.(Z)/JG 5 (Wk-Nrs. 3528 and 2547) were seriously damaged. Both were able to make emergency landings at their airfield, but they were later written off. One could have been the Bf 110 credited to Kurzenkov.

At noon that same day 12 Hurricanes drawn from 2nd GKAP and 78th IAP provided an escort for six I-153 attack aircraft. The formation was intercepted close to the target area by Bf 109Fs of 6./JG 5, which attacked the slow-moving biplanes head-on and broke up their formation. The German fighters then re-formed into pairs to set upon individual I-153s. Three were quickly downed, killing one pilot and seriously wounding two others. Only four Hurricanes from the escort group engaged the enemy, as according to a report from the Commander-in-Chief of the Northern Fleet Air Force, the rest of the covering force was 'distracted from their principal objective by enemy aircraft'. Put simply, there was a lack of coordination between escort and escorted.

Among those who did 'carry out his principal objective' and engage the enemy fighters was Pavel Orlov. He attacked a Bf 109 from behind and poured two long bursts of machine gun fire into it. The pilot later reported that 'the aircraft caught fire and fell towards the ground'. This victory, however, remained unconfirmed. Based on the final results of this air battle, Orlov was awarded his first military honour in the form of the Order of the Red Banner, a decoration his squadronmate Sergey Kurzenkov had received earlier in the month.

During a sortie on 9 May to intercept enemy aircraft, Orlov and Kurzenkov each reported shooting down a Bf 109 in a confrontation with single- and twin-engined fighters escorting Ju 87s that were targeting troops in the Soviet frontline. Orlov led five Hurricanes from the 2nd Squadron, while Kurzenkov joined a group of four led by the 3rd Squadron's Guards Capt Shvedov. While manoeuvring during the aerial battle, Guards Sgt Savin from Orlov's group collided with Shvedov's Hurricane and cut off its tail. Both aircraft crashed to the ground, taking their pilots with them.

Orlov and Kurzenkov were lucky to survive the next day's difficult and bloody confrontation with the 'polar hunters' of JG 5. Troops of the 12th Independent Marine Brigade had suffered heavy losses in an encounter with German alpine troops, and lacking reserves, they were down to 100-150 combat-capable soldiers. In an effort to annihilate the remaining Soviet troops, the Luftwaffe pounded their defensive positions with three raids of 20-25 aircraft. The Marine Brigade commander called

Northern Fleet headquarters requesting help and the Northern Fleet Air Force command responded by scrambling all available fighters and despatching attack aircraft to strike the enemy troops.

In the first hour after dawn on 10 May the weather over the battlefield improved, and enemy bombers were reported to be heading for the frontline with a fighter escort. A total of 23 Hurricanes from 78th IAP and 2nd GKAP were scrambled immediately from Vaenga-1 and Vaenga-2 airfields. The first to arrive over the front were 14 78th IAP Hurricanes, flying at a height of about 2000 m (6500 ft). They were followed by two groups from the Guards unit flying at the same altitude. While they were en route to the target area the Soviet pilots sighted ten Bf 110s and six Bf 109s slightly above them, but still under the cloud base. The Guards pilots attacked with RS-82 rocket projectiles, the official report on the action later recalling that 'Despite the numerical advantage of the Soviet forces, the enemy aircraft did not scatter in a panic but attempted to launch a counter-attack'.

The Soviet pilots responded according to their well-rehearsed plan, with groups of Hurricanes forming three defensive circles at 2000 m, 1500 m and 500 m (6500 ft, 5000 ft and 1600 ft) to repel the German machines. Flying outside the circle singly or in pairs, the Luftwaffe fighters attempted to sneak out of the clouds and catch the Soviet pilots unawares. Meanwhile, some had broken off to escort the bombers back to their base.

At the risk of being pounced upon by the waiting German aircraft, Kurzenkov decided to break out of the circle and mount a single-handed attack. As two Bf 110s and three Bf 109s targeted the circle, he fired at a Bf 110 from a range of 250 m. Leaving the circle, he tried to attack a lone Bf 109, whose pilot attempted to evade him by making shallow turns to prevent Kurzenkov getting him in his sights. The Soviet pilot

Also fitted with Soviet cannon and machine guns, this Hurricane IIB taxies out at the start of another sortie during the spring of 1942

then became the quarry as he came under fire from another German fighter. Breaking off his attack, he turned sharply away and then went into a steep dive. At this point Kurzenkov spotted another Bf 109 diving in front of him. Latching onto its tail, he fired two bursts but then ran out of ammunition. The German fighter levelled off, but immediately came under a head-on attack from another Hurricane. Then, according to Kurzenkov, the Bf 109 flew into a hill and exploded. Its destruction, however, was attributed to Kurzenkov, who was able to add the fighter to his score.

Pilots of 78th IAP also distinguished themselves in this battle by claiming the destruction of two Bf 109s and a Bf 110, one of the single-engined fighters being added to Sgibnev's tally. The official report states that he 'attacked a single Me 109 from the rear from a range of 100 m and opened fire with four machine guns. The aircraft went into a steep dive before crashing somewhere near Malaya Zapadnaya Litsa'. The report added that Sgibnev's aircraft suffered damage to its cooling and lubrication systems.

The cost for 78th IAP was a high one. Three Hurricanes were shot down and their pilots, Snr Lt I L Zhivotovskiy, Lt V I Bukharin and Sgt E A Evstegneev, were killed. Two more pilots were forced to make emergency landings in their damaged aircraft. Despite these losses, the total number of victories attributed that day to Northern Fleet pilots was two Bf 110s and four Bf 109s.

Two hours after this battle had been fought the Guards pilots were back in the air, nine Hurricanes in two groups escorting five SB bombers to the frontline. The first group was led by Kurzenkov, while Orlov headed up the second, the escorting fighters flying above and to the right of the bombers. On their way to the target they were told that a large number of enemy aircraft were awaiting their arrival. Moments after they had received this radio warning from the regimental command post, the Soviet pilots sighted ten Bf 110s heading for them at a higher altitude. Behind them, approaching out of the sun, were several flights of Bf 109s. The enemy fighters broke up into groups and pairs and then proceeded to attack the bombers in a pincer movement.

Orlov's fighters met the Bf 110s head-on, which was a brave move as each of the German machines had two 20 mm cannon and four 7.92 mm machine guns in the nose. Although some of the Hurricanes were fitted with 20 mm ShVAK cannon and 12.7 mm heavy machine guns, most were armed with 7.7 mm Brownings. The Soviet Hurricanes were clearly at a disadvantage as the opposing fighters rushed towards each other. The consequences were inevitable, with two Hurricanes being immediately shot down and their pilots, Guards Capt L L Mozerov

Seven-victory Hurricane ace Snr Lt Aleksey Dizhevskiy poses with his fighter at Vaenga-2 airfield in the spring of 1942. Note the aircraft's unusual combination of weapons – two ShVAK 20 mm cannon and two BK 12.7 mm and four Colt-Browning 7.7 mm machine guns, all mounted in the wings. When configured in this way, the Hurricane packed the heaviest punch of any fighter then in service in the USSR

and Guards Snr Lt V V Kravchenko, killed. Orlov, however, avoided the fire poured out from the Bf 110s by making a series of violent turns, although he became separated from the rest of his group and lost sight of them in the process. His lone fighter was quickly pounced on by a Bf 109, although Orlov managed to shake it off with difficulty before returning home at low level. He was the only member of his formation to make it back to Vaenga-2.

Meanwhile, having fired at the Hurricanes, the pilots of the Bf 110s backed off to give the German flak batteries an opportunity to engage the Soviet bombers. The twin-engined fighters then gained height and headed back into the sun. With the enemy fighters in a good tactical position for a second attack, the SB bombers abandoned their mission, jettisoned their bombs and headed for home. By this time Kurzenkov had already ordered his fighters to attack the Bf 110s head-on so as to provide cover for the departing bombers. The official report states that 'Guards Snr Lt Kurzenkov attacked a group of Me 110s and did not return to the formation. He was hit and made an emergency landing'.

In his memoirs Sergey Kurzenkov recalled the consequences of this deadly head-on attack;

'The enemy fighters rushed past. A flame from my damaged wing was fanned by the airflow. I tried to land but the speed was slightly above the normal landing speed. There was a narrow gorge, and sheer dark mountain faces were in front of me. I managed to pull the control column towards me. The aircraft cleared the cliff. My eyes searched hurriedly for another gorge. There it was to the left – a small corrective turn and that's where I planned to land, but then I decided I wasn't going to land there. I would hit granite at the end of my landing roll. I put the aircraft into a side-slip to starboard once again, and this time I hit the ground. Impact! I don't remember anything else.

'Overcoming dizziness, I tried to get to my feet but something was stopping me. Damn it! I still had my parachute on, but the seat harness was dangling above me. Releasing it, I tried to remove my parachute. I climbed out with difficulty and, to my surprise, I found that I'd been thrown 20 m from the wreckage of the aircraft. Ploughing through the snow, I approached the aircraft. All that was left were sorry remains. Sharp, splintered pieces of bonded wood instead of an airscrew were sticking out like horns. The port wing had become corrugated and resembled a set of elongated bellows. The starboard wing was lopsided and the duralumin had become blackened by smoke, with ragged, gaping holes in it. The engine had sheared its bolts and the whole cylinder block had gone into the cockpit, splitting the dashboard and pushing the control column tightly against the seat. I involuntarily shuddered upon seeing this. What would have become of me if I hadn't been thrown from the cockpit?

'Standing on the wing and looking at the shattered cockpit, I glanced into the round mirror fixed to the upper part of the canopy behind the windscreen. I was horrified by what I saw – there was a gaping wound on my forehead close to my left temple. Blood was pouring down my face, and my left eye socket was a solid, bloody mess. It was no joke. I was scared, as I thought that my eye had been knocked out. However, I touched my eye carefully and relaxed, as it still seemed to be intact.

Reaching for a bandage, I cleaned the clotted blood away from my left eye and covered the right one with the palm of my hand. But for a light, misty haze, my vision was much as it had been before I crash-landed.

'I jumped into the snow and walked up to the fuselage, which had been torn off, as had the tail section. There was a first aid box in there with a packet of food and some skis with sticks – everything I urgently needed. However, there was almost nothing left. Cotton wool had spread like hoarfrost throughout the fuselage and fragments from exploding cannon shells had shredded the bandages, although fortunately the flask of iodine had survived. Cylindrical in shape, it was made from thick, unbreakable glass. I administered first aid in front of the round mirror, then I reached for the food pack. The tins of meat had been peppered with bullets, one having passed through five layers of chocolate before becoming embedded in the sixth. As far as the biscuits were concerned, they had turned into ground-up rusks!

'I decided to take some refreshment. I took the flask from my pocket and poured myself a few gulps of cognac and ate the half bars of chocolate, but I felt no better. I got into the skis with difficulty and, taking the remains of the food pack with me, as well as rockets and a flare gun, I checked the compass and set off to the east through the virgin snow. The untouched whiteness was painful to my injured left eye.'

Two other pilots from the escort group, Guards Snr Sgt P D Klimov and Guards Sgt M M Chepurnov, had their Hurricanes badly shot up as well, but they also managed to crash-land their crippled aircraft on the tundra and return to their unit on foot. Above them, the three remaining Hurricanes continued to cover the five bombers, repelling the attacks by German fighters. The Bf 109 pilots gave up after a few fruitless attacks, but several Bf 110 crews stubbornly chased the Soviet aircraft as far as the Kola Gulf.

Thanks to the efforts of the Hurricane pilots, none of the SBs suffered any damage in this hard-fought engagement. The guards pilots had done their duty right to the very end of the mission, preventing the Messerschmitts from getting anywhere near their charges. The price, though, had been high. Of the nine Hurricanes that took part in the operation, only four made it back home. For the whole of the Northern Fleet Air Force the day's losses totalled nine Hurricanes and five pilots. The Bf 110 crews claimed to have shot down 16 Soviet fighters without loss. For their part, the guards pilots reported shooting down five enemy aircraft. Guards Capt Mozerov, Capt Orlov and Snr Lt Kurzenkov each claimed a Bf 110 apiece, while Guards Snr Lt Kravchenko and Guards Sgt Klimov were credited with a Bf 109 each. German sources, however, admitted only the loss of Bf 109E-7 Wk-Nr. 5975, which, along with its pilot Unteroffizier Heinz Bausch, disappeared without trace.

Three high-scoring aces of 2nd GKAP, Northern Fleet Air Force, come together during a photo opportunity in early 1943. They are, from left to right, Capts Pavel Orlov, and Aleksander Kovalenko and Snr Lt Vladimir Pokrovskiy. The latter was credited with 11 victories in total, three of them in Hurricanes. His remaining successes came in the I-16 and P-40

10 May also saw the military council of the Northern Fleet recommend that Guards Capt Aleksander Kovalenko, CO of 2nd GKAB's 2nd Squadron, be awarded the title of HSU in recognition of his 12 victories, the last five of which made him a Northern Fleet Air Force Hurricane ace. By then Kovalenko had flown 146 combat sorties and participated in 22 aerial engagements. His award was dated 14 June 1942 by order of the Presidium of the Supreme Soviet.

Death of Orlov

Meanwhile, Sergey Kurzenkov was in hospital recovering from the head injury he sustained during his forced landing. By the end of May, when he returned to duty, his eight victories still put him one up on his rival, and comrade, Pavel Orlov. The latter was to receive the Order of the Red Banner at the beginning of June, but his time as a Hurricane pilot was now coming to an end. His next battles would be fought with American fighters, namely the Kittyhawk I and P-39N Airacobra.

By the end of January 1943 Orlov was a squadron leader, and he had just claimed his 11th enemy aircraft while flying a P-39. However, on 15 March the Hurricane ace fought his last battle. He was one of a number of Northern Fleet pilots searching for a comrade who had failed to return from a sortie the previous evening. Flying low over enemy territory, they encountered a formation of Bf 109Fs that had an altitude advantage over the Soviet fighters. After the initial attack, the P-39 pilots broke up and the fight continued as a series of individual battles. It was a confused situation, and none of his comrades could later say exactly how Orlov had met his death. Two days later a search party found his crashed aircraft on the tundra, the dead ace being discovered in the cockpit of his P-39. His logbook recorded 329 operational sorties, during which he had fought in 32 aerial battles. Orlov was also credited with destroying 12 enemy aircraft.

He was posthumously awarded the title of HSU by order of the Presidium of the Supreme Soviet, dated 24 July 1943. The official recommendation had noted in particular that 'There was a confidence in the regiment, with good reason, that wherever Capt Orlov and his subordinates were engaged in combat they would surely be victorious over the enemy'.

As his regimental colleague and fellow HSU Zakhar Sorokhin recalled after the war;

'I can still see him standing before me even now, heavy set with broad shoulders. He looked somehow clumsy on the ground, yet in the air he was distinguished by his exceptional skill and decisiveness. We always watched his masterly flights with excitement. It seemed he was born to be a fighter pilot.'

This sombre photograph was taken at the funeral of Capt Pavel Orlov, who was killed in aerial combat on 15 March 1943. In the guard of honour, to the right, is his brother officer, friend and ace Capt Vladimir Pokrovskiy

ARCTIC WAR HOTS UP

From March 1942 the Arctic air war grew more and more intense as the weather improved. Luftwaffe bombers pounded the port of Murmansk and the raids became more ferocious with each passing day. It seemed as though the Germans were trying to force a conclusion to the campaign. Previous raids had targeted the port and shipping in the Kola Gulf, but now it was the city itself that was coming under attack. By May the pilots of JG 5 *Eismeer* had adopted the tactic of 'clearing the skies' over Murmansk in advance of the dive-bombers' arrival. A few minutes before the Stukas commenced their diving attacks, Bf 109s would appear over the target and engage the patrolling Soviet fighters, enabling the Ju 87s to deliver their ordnance virtually unopposed. The Messerschmitt pilots were also active over Soviet airfields, waiting for the fighters to return.

It was during these difficult conditions for Soviet pilots that a new star emerged. Snr Lt Petr Sgibnev commanded the 1st Squadron of 78th IAP. Just 21 years of age, he would become the highest scoring surviving ace of the polar theatre of operations following the death of the top Northern Fleet ace Boris Safonov on 30 May 1942 while defending the Allied convoy PQ-16.

The highest scoring ace of JG 5 *Eismeer* during 1942 was Feldwebel Rudolf Müller. He was considered the top Hurricane-killer of the polar front, and he developed the risky tactic of breaking the defensive circle formed by Soviet pilots on encountering a force of Bf 109s. Credited with 92 victories in total, Müller's Hurricane tally stood at 35. He was forced down on the frozen surface of Lake Bolschoje following combat with 30-40 Soviet fighters over Murmansk on 19 April 1943 and subsequently captured. He later perished in captivity

That month, prior to his death, Safonov had reported shooting down five enemy aircraft, and Petr Sgibnev had recorded his tenth victory.

On 30 May a Luftwaffe strike force of Ju 88s from II./KG 30, escorted by a large force of Bf 109s and Bf 110s, targeted vessels of PQ-16 whilst they were at anchor in Kola Gulf. A total of 37 Soviet fighters from the Northern Fleet Air Force, the 14th Air Army and 122nd IAD took off to intercept them. Although some of the enemy bombers were scattered by Soviet fighters, individual Ju 88s managed to break through the dense anti-aircraft fire and the fighter shield to drop their bombs. Most fell into the water and exploded harmlessly, but one 500 kg (1100 lb) bomb detonated near the 6187-ton American vessel *Deer Lodge*, damaging its hull. The ship remained afloat, but had to be given assistance to move to shallow water.

The Northern Fleet pilots, together with a group of 13 Hurricanes from 78th IAP, intercepted six Ju 88s and two Bf 110s. According to Northern Fleet Air Force Headquarters operations report No 0138 of 19 May 1942;

'Sgibnev attacked one Ju 88 from above and behind, opening fire with four machine guns from a distance of 300-100 m. The aircraft caught fire and crashed near lake Kilp-Yavr. Babiy attacked another Ju 88 from above and behind, opening fire with four to five long bursts from a distance of 200-100 m. The aircraft entered a steep dive and crashed into the ground six kilometres [four miles] southwest of Lake Dolgoe. Bershanskiy attacked a Ju 88 from directly behind its tail and opened fire with five bursts. The aircraft caught fire and crashed five kilometres [three miles] south of Kyadel-Yavr. Doroshin shot down a Ju 88 and Dilanyan shot down a single Me 110. The fall of these aircraft is confirmed by air defence posts and verified from the air by the regimental commander.'

78th IAP pilots participating in this battle claimed four Ju 88s and a Bf 110 destroyed. At the same time the pilots of 122nd IAD and the 14th Army Air Force, who also played a part in countering the raid,

Sgt N D Bryzzhanov of 769th IAP, 122nd IAD of the Air Defence Forces hit a tractor while landing on 20 March 1942. Note the RAF presentation titling *SKYLARK II* just aft of the cockpit

High-scoring Hurricane ace Aleksey Dizhevskiy was born in 1917 in Kronshtadt, near Leningrad. Twenty years later he entered Eysk Naval Aviation School. In 1940 he was posted to 72nd SAP of the Northern Fleet Air Force as a junior pilot in a squadron equipped with I-15bis biplane fighters. Dizhevskiy converted to the Hurricane in early 1942 with 2nd GSAP. After the re-organisation of the Northern Fleet Air Force in March 1942, Dizhevskiy served with 78th IAP as a deputy squadron commander. His first victory was achieved on 4 April 1942, and in May 1943 Dizhevskiy was appointed to lead 27th IAP. By war's end he was CO of 41st IAP, Pacific Fleet Air Force. Dizhevskiy was awarded the Order of the Red Banner three times

claimed to have destroyed 13 Ju 88s, although, as was often the case, the reality was very different. Indeed, KG 30 lost only Ju 88A-4 Wk-Nr. 1746.

After the battle Sgibnev was awarded his second Order of the Red Banner, and also recommended to receive the title of HSU. The official citation that accompanied the latter read as follows;

'For the whole period of the war with the German invaders up to now, comrade Sgibnev has flown 260 combat sorties, totalling 243 hr 40 min flying time. He has engaged in 21 air battles, during which he has personally shot down ten enemy aircraft. One of Stalin's original falcons, Comrade Pilot Sgibnev is consistently contributing to the glory of our Great Motherland. Through his indomitable ambition he seeks a fight with the enemy, and on finding it, he is unfailingly victorious.'

In mid May another 21-year-old pilot and flight commander, Lt Vasiliy Doroshin, began making a name for himself too, despite having been fighting as a member of the Northern Fleet Air Force since the first days of the war. He reported destroying three enemy aircraft (a Bf 110, a Bf 109 and a Ju 88) in the space of one week. Doroshin's first success came on 12 May during a sortie to repel another raid on Murmansk, and he claimed his second aircraft the following day. His third victory came on 18 May.

There was no let-up in the intensity of the battles in the skies over Murmansk during June. Sgibnev increased his score with two kills, but it was his regimental colleague and deputy squadron commander Snr Lt Aleksey Dizhevskiy who achieved the month's greatest number of victories. Among the three enemy aircraft he claimed to have destroyed were a pair of Ju 87s during a single raid on the 2nd. That morning the Luftwaffe struck twice at Murmansk and its port. The Northern Fleet Air Force scrambled 30 fighters at 1120 hrs to repel the first raid, which comprised nine Ju 87s escorted by four Bf 109s and a similar number of Bf 110s. Several jetties were seriously damaged as well as the railway line to the port. A submarine, which was under repair in the shipyard, was also damaged by a bomb.

The Hurricanes were joined by a squadron of I-16s under the command of Capt Vasiliy Adonkin. The Polikarpov pilots engaged the Bf 109s, giving their compatriots in the Hurricanes an opportunity to attack the enemy bombers without interference. Snr Lt Dizhevskiy, who was leading six Hurricanes, subsequently reported;

'We were patrolling over Mishukov Cape airfield when we encountered eight or nine Ju 87s at 1125 hrs at an altitude of 3500 m [11,375 ft]. They were flying out of the cloud and out of the sun on a bombing mission. I called on my group to close up and we attacked head-on and from below as a group. Having prevented the enemy aircraft from diving on their targets, they lost altitude and attempted to turn for home. This was a mistake, as their manoeuvring allowed us to get in behind them and continue the pursuit.

'I attacked two Ju 87s, the first from behind and below. I fired two bursts into its engine and the Stuka started to smoke. Dropping onto its port wing, the aircraft went down vertically in flames. I then attacked a second Ju 87. I caught up with it and attacked from below and behind from a distance of 30-20 m. After I had used up all my ammunition, I watched as the Ju 87's engine cowlings broke loose and the engine started to smoke heavily. The aircraft disappeared in a steep dive east of Lake Pyayve-Yavr. I was not able to pursue the dive-bombers any further because of an Me 110, which I engaged in combat. Following this battle I landed safely at my home airfield. My aircraft was undamaged.'

The victories reported by Aleksey Dizhevskiy represented the third and fourth he had scored while flying the Hurricane, and following this success he was promoted to the rank of captain. In all, the pilots of 78th IAP claimed to have destroyed ten enemy aircraft during the 2 June raid. This total was comprised of six Ju 87s, three Bf 109s and a single Bf 110. German sources state that 3./StG 5 lost only two Ju 87Rs (Wk-Nrs. 5485 and 5545) and had three crewmen killed (Oberleutnant Karl Pauls, Unteroffizier Jakob Holtmaier and Leutnant Karl Rapp). Air gunner

On 2 June 1942, while repelling an air raid on the port of Murmansk, the pilots of the Northern Fleet Air Force reported shooting down ten enemy aircraft. Pictured here are 78th IAP Hurricane aces Snr Lt Vasiliy Doroshin (right), who claimed a Bf 109 to add to his score, and Snr Lt Dizhevskiy (left), who shot down two Ju 87s

Ju 87Bs of I./StG 5 were routinely engaged by Hurricanes over Murmansk in 1942. When Soviet fighter pilots managed to find a gap in the fighter escort, these dive-bombers became easy prey

Obergefreiter Werner Somann survived being shot down and was taken prisoner. Under interrogation, he made the following observation;

'It has become more difficult to get away from the enemy fighters recently, in as much as now the Russian pilots are starting to get as close as 7-10 m from the bombers, which previously didn't happen.'

Judging by Somann's statement, the Northern Fleet pilots had started to get in much closer to the German dive-bombers before opening fire.

The loss of two dive-bombers, together with their crews, was a significant success for the pilots of the Northern Fleet, especially as they had suffered no losses in return. The following pilots from 78th IAP were amongst those who claimed to have destroyed a Ju 87 – Snr Lt Sgibnev (his 12th victory), Lt I M Dilonyan (his third victory), P L Kolomiets (his third victory), Lt N I Nikolayev (his second victory) and Sgt A M Pilipenko (his first victory). Even Hurricane ace V S Doroshin increased

Aces of 2nd GKAP say farewell to brother officers being sent on leave during the autumn of 1942. Second from left is Aleksey Dizhevskiy, whilst immediately behind him (also in a flying helmet) is future HSU Petr Kolomiets – he claimed the first three of his 13 victories in the Hurricane, with the remaining ten coming at the controls of a P-39

This Hurricane from 2nd GKAP displays the legend 'Learn how to kill the vermin in Safonov's style!' Such messages painted on the fuselages of Soviet fighters were common in the Northern Fleet Air Force from the first weeks of the war in the east

his score when he reported shooting down a Bf 109. This earned him a second Order of the Red Banner to add to the first awarded on 22 February 1942.

It was not such a successful day for the pilots of 2nd GKAP, however. Seven Hurricanes, led by Aleksey Kovalenko, were sent aloft to counter the second raid on Murmansk's port, but they suffered heavy losses. Three Hurricanes (BH328, Z5052 and Z5252) were shot down and Guards Sgt A V Vanyukhin was killed. Only a solitary Bf 109 was claimed by Guards Lt P P Markov in return, although this was not confirmed.

Dizhevskiy and Doroshin both increased their scores on 13 June when eight Northern Fleet Hurricanes were scrambled to intercept Ju 87s. Their pilots, however, encountered an escort group of seven Bf 109s, which they engaged. According to participants' reports, Dizhevskiy, Doroshin, Snr Lt Nikolayev and Lt Vasiliy Shalaev all claimed their third victories, although the latter was subsequently shot down. Having

Ju 88 bombers of KG 30 succeeded in destroying two-thirds of Murmansk's houses (which were of timber construction) on 18 June 1942, the city's residential area being devastated by incendiary bombs dropped in AB 1000 containers

suffered a slight foot wound, Shalaev took to his parachute and landed safely.

On 1 July an aerial clash involving pilots of 78th IAP, led by Capt Sgibnev, became one of the most significant in the history of the Northern Fleet Air Force. Seven Hurricanes from the regiment repelled a raid by Ju 87s, the Soviet pilots claiming to have downed seven of nine dive-bombers engaged without loss. The Germans, however, stated that only two aircraft were destroyed, Ju 87Rs' Wk-Nrs. 5691 and 6225. The aircrew involved, Leutnant Leo Schobert, Unteroffizier Arno Jansen, Feldwebel August Greiner and Unteroffizier Wolfgang Ossowski, were all killed.

Ranking Soviet Hurricane ace Snr Lt Petr Sgibnev was the youngest squadron commander in the Northern Fleet Air Force, being appointed leader of the first squadron of 78th IAP on 18 June 1942 when he was just 21

A detailed description of this encounter has survived, and an analysis of the reports reveal the actions of the pilots themselves and the tactics employed by the Northern Fleet Air Force during this crucial period in the defence of Murmansk. The official 78th IAP account noted that at 1850 hrs its pilots were patrolling over the port of Murmansk at an altitude of 4000 m (13,000 ft);

A Northern Fleet anti-aircraft artillery position defending the port of Murmansk. It was common practice during the summer of 1942 for Hurricane pilots to retreat behind an anti-aircraft barrage when encountering enemy fighters in the Murmansk area so as to save themselves for attacks on the raiding bombers

'Performing a barrel roll over the port, the pilots noticed a series of explosions from anti-aircraft artillery shells, indicating the direction from which the enemy aircraft were approaching. The leader of the group, Petr Sgibnev, sighted nine Ju 87s approaching at an altitude of 3000 m [10,000 ft]. The leading group decided to attack the dive-bombers head-on. As a result of the first attack the dive-bombers dropped their bombs in the mountains. They turned and, descending one by one, set course for their own territory. Having dispersed their opponents, the Soviet pilots continued to attack the fleeing dive-bombers from close range.

'In his first head-on attack, Capt Sgibnev fired five to six bursts of machine gun fire from a distance of 300-100 m at a Ju 87. The dive-bomber caught fire and went down. Having disposed of one Ju 87, Capt Sgibnev caught up with another. He attacked it from above and behind from a distance of 50-30 m. The enemy aircraft started to descend haphazardly after two bursts of machine gun fire. The crewmembers bailed out. One was shot in the air by Soviet pilots but the other landed safely.'

The following pilots each claimed to have shot down a Ju 87 – Capt Babiy (his fifth victory), Capt Dizhevskiy (his sixth), Snr Lt Shalaev (his fifth) and Lt Dilanyan (his fourth), while Sgibnev claimed two for his 14th and 15th aerial victories.

It was also during this battle that Konstantin Babiy and Vasiliy Shalaev became Northern Fleet Hurricane aces. Judging by their reports, they both downed their Stukas during the first attack. They would receive the Order of the Red Banner on 23 July for their successes. This was in fact the second time Babiy had been presented with the award, his first being issued on 22 February 1942.

Much of the credit for the success of the Northern Fleet pilots on this occasion belongs to their squadron commander, Capt Petr Sgibnev. The following statement describing the leading role he played in dispersing the enemy attack was contained in an official 78th IAP report;

'As a result of well-organised observation by the Hurricane pilots, the enemy dive-bombers were immediately intercepted and attacked vigorously. Having lost their leader in the first attack, the dive-bombers scattered and started to depart one by one in a panic, the gunners hardly firing a shot. The personal example of the leader of the group, Capt Sgibnev,

Also enjoying great success as a Hurricane pilot, Konstantin Babiy was born in 1917 to a peasant family in the village of Sovyetskoe, in the Zhitomir Region of Ukraine, in 1936 he graduated from Pedagogical Secondary School, and the following year Babiy entered Eysk Naval Aviation School. In 1940 he was posted to 72nd SAP of the Northern Fleet Air Force as a junior pilot. Initially seeing combat in a squadron equipped with I-15bis, he converted to the Hurricane in early 1942 with 2nd GSAP and scored the first of his seven Hurricane victories on 15 April that same year. When the conflict ended Babiy was a squadron commander with 54th SAP, White Sea Air Fleet Air Force. He received the Order of the Red Banner three times

together with the positive results of the first attack, instilled yet more confidence in the pilots that the bombers could be routed.'

But further analysis of the actions of Northern Fleet pilots during this engagement highlights not only an inefficient use of their fighters, but also the weakness of tactical training at that time, even among more experienced squadron commanders. The accounts also reveal that the defending fighter pilots only became aware of the approach of enemy bombers when they saw bursting anti-aircraft shells surrounding the formation. This proves that in the summer of 1942 the Northern Fleet air defence system was still not making full use of the radios fitted in the Hurricanes to vector them towards hostile aircraft once they had been seen by Red Army spotters in the field.

The Soviet pilots' head-on attacks, which were used to break up the Ju 87 formation, represented the classic opening gambit of air combat on the eastern front throughout 1942. This was followed by numerous independent actions, implying that individual pilots were then set free to pursue enemy bombers. Such a tactic usually led to heavy losses of Soviet fighters and pilots when the dive-bombers' fighter escorts reacted to the Hurricanes' attack. On this particular occasion, however, Sgibnev's pilots were lucky. They were soon joined by other Hurricanes from 122nd IAD that were able to keep the escorting fighters occupied, although the Northern Fleet pilots had failed to spot six Bf 109s that were following the Ju 87s at a different altitude.

It should be said at this point that in 1942 Northern Fleet fighter pilots were still employing the tactics developed by Boris Safonov during his early battles with German bombers in the summer of 1941 – a

A victim of Vaenga-2 based Hurricanes, this Ju 87R of I./StG 5 crashed near Murmansk in the early summer of 1942

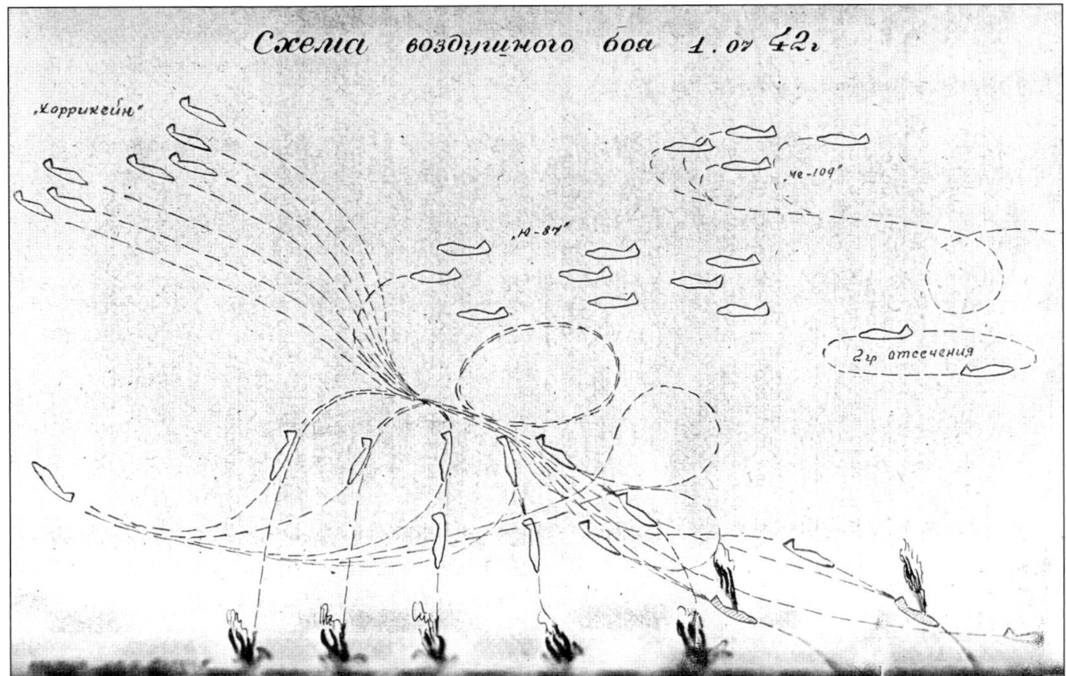

This diagram illustrates the battle on 1 July 1942 when 78th IAP pilots, led by Petr Sgibnev, reported the destruction of seven Ju 87 dive-dombers that were attempting to target Murmansk

surprise formation attack followed by the selection of opponents by individual pilots. The tactic worked well enough in 1941, when German bombers generally operated in the Murmansk area without fighter escort.

In the case of the 1 July 1942 battle, six pilots each claimed to have shot down an enemy bomber and three of the leading group claimed two. Clearly a sudden mass attack like this had an impact on the morale of enemy bomber crews, but the tactic also exposed the Soviet fighter pilots to attack by the escorting fighters, although in mid-1942 such a head-on pass was still considered a valid tactic. Yet alongside the reference to the successful and 'well-organised action as a group', there was some criticism of the Hurricanes' leader in the official report of the battle;

'Capt Sgibnev made a fundamental mistake by being so engrossed in his pursuit of the enemy that he failed to organise a re-grouping of his pilots after the battle, which resulted in them returning to their airfield individually.'

At a conference of Northern Fleet pilots held shortly after the 1 July action, Sgibnev shared his observations and experiences from the battle with his colleagues;

'There is no need to be afraid of attacking a Ju 87 head-on, as it is defenceless from an attack from this direction. However, it is difficult to aim during a head-on attack, and firing can therefore be ineffective. One has to know the weak points of enemy aircraft, and hit them there. The Me 109 is a good aircraft, but even it has a weak spot. In the Hurricane, you cannot get away from the Messerschmitt in level flight. Nevertheless, it can be shot down if you manage to get behind the fighter, as it is not a strong aircraft. It is also lightly armed with one cannon and two machine guns. Me 109 pilots never enter into head-on attacks.'

Two days after the 1 July clash, four 78th IAP Hurricanes, together with a flight of I-15bis fighters from 27th IAP, intercepted a formation

This Hurricane from an unidentified regiment forced-landed following engine failure. The main cause of the problems that afflicted the aircraft's Merlin XX engine in 1942 was the fighter's operation from sandy airfields without dust filters

of enemy aircraft that was comprised of seven Ju 87s escorted by six Bf 109s and four Bf 110s. Upon returning from the sortie Capt Babiy and Snr Lt Loginov each reported downing a Ju 87.

These successes in the skies over Murmansk in early July would prove to be the last for 78th IAP, as the number of combat-ready foreign-built aircraft was declining with each passing day. The Hurricanes in particular suffered from the dust and sand encountered on the airfields from which they operated, these conditions reducing the service lives of their Merlin XX engines to around 20 to 30 hours when run without dust filters. To ensure that the surviving Hurricanes were used more effectively, the Northern Fleet command was forced to temporarily transfer all the British-made fighters to a single regiment, 78th IAP, in early July. Even so, the regiment was seldom capable of fielding more than eight to ten combat-worthy aircraft on any one day. On 22 July, for example, there were only nine serviceable fighters out of 50 on the combined strength of the regiment's three squadrons. A similar situation persisted through to the end of 1942 among the fighter units based on the Kola Peninsula.

The offensive capacity of the Hurricane regiments deteriorated markedly during the second half of 1942, and this situation was reflected in the memoirs of the air defence pilots of 768th IAP of 122nd IAD. In a letter to the author dated 12 March 1985, ace Georgiy Ivanovich Kozlov described his first battle as a Hurricane pilot in the Murmansk area in the summer of 1942;

'There were a great many aircraft from both sides in a German raid on the port and on Murmansk itself. There were only a handful of us in Hurricanes, however, due to a lack of serviceable aircraft. My squadronmates went after the enemy bombers, but failed to warn me that they were doing so. In the heat of battle I didn't immediately notice that I was alone at my height, although the German fighter escorts did.

All the Hurricane IIs supplied by No 151 Wing RAF directly to 78th IAP were equipped with chin-mounted dust filters when they arrived at Vaenga-1 airfield

When operating from sandy frontline Soviet airfields without a dust filter (as in this case), the service life of a brand new Merlin XX engine could be reduced from 240 hours to as few as 40 hours. Indeed, in some cases these engines failed after little more than 30 hours of flying

Most damaged or crashed Hurricanes in Red Army Air Force service were cannibalised for much needed spares in 1942

After the mass failure of Merlin XX engines due to operations from sandy airfields without dust filters in the summer of 1942, Northern Fleet Air Force technicians hastily designed this air filter during the winter of 1942-43. It was subsequently used with success

They were soon attacking me from all sides, tracer passing right beside me, literally a metre away. My situation was becoming critical. A I Shvetsov was constantly giving me orders over the radio from 122nd IAD's command post, but I just didn't have time to react to them. I had only one life-saving thought in these few moments – to throw the aircraft into a spin. That's what I did. When I recovered the Hurricane I could see that there were a large number of our aircraft in the "carousel" below me, from the Northern Fleet Air Force, the 14th Army Air Force and our own air defence aircraft.'

Death of Petr Sgibnev

Having displayed his skill and courage during the aerial battles fought during the spring and summer of 1942, Petr Sgibnev progressed rapidly through the ranks. At the beginning of October he was posted to 2nd GKAP and on the 13th of that month was awarded the title of HSU. He also received a Gold Star as well as the Order of Lenin by order of the Presidium of the Supreme Soviet. By the end of the year Sgibnev's achievements had been recognised by the Allies, and he received a British DFC.

In January 1943 Sgibnev succeeded Guards Maj Ivan Tumanov as the commander of 2nd GKAB after the latter was killed in an aircraft accident – this unit had previously been led by

The duty pilots of 2nd GKAP in the Lenin room at Vaenga-2, which was reserved for political discussion . . . and chess!

Boris Safonov. For the next few months Sgibnev continued to fly Hurricanes, despite the presence of more modern P-39s and Kittyhawk Is within his new command. Following a sortie on 26 February he claimed to have shot down an enemy aircraft in a running battle with two Bf 109s, but this was not officially confirmed.

78th IAP's Maj Petr Sgibnev explains to Snr Lt Sergey Loginov how he claimed his latest victory after their return from a successful mission to intercept enemy aircraft attacking Murmansk in the spring of 1943. Loginov claimed three of his five victories flying Hurricanes with 78th IAP and 2nd GKAP

Pictured here during the spring of 1943 are (from left to right) the CO of 2nd GKAP, Maj P G Sgibnev, deputy CO for flying training, Maj A N Kukharenko, regimental commissar F P Pronyakov and head of regimental staff, Maj I F Antonov

Eventually, Sgibnev switched to the Airacobra, and it was while flying the Bell fighter that he filed his final three claims, for Bf 109s shot down, to take his score to 19. Then, during a training flight on 3 May, he performed a 'climbing roll' at too low an altitude and perished when his P-39 crashed. For several decades after the war, however, official documents insisted that Guards Maj Petr Sgibnev had met his death in battle.

Curiously, most of the Northern Fleet pilots who had distinguished themselves during the first half of 1942 faded into obscurity in 1943. One such individual was Konstantin Babiy. By November 1942 his various successes earlier in the year had seen him promoted to lead the 1st Hurricane squadron of 78th IAP, but between then and June 1943 he added only one victory (a Bf 109) to his score. Babiy was subsequently sent on training courses to gain further qualifications, returning to the Northern Fleet Air Force in January 1944. He then completed further spells in command of various squadrons within 78th IAP and 54th SAP of the White Sea Flotilla Air Force through to war's end. Babiy served post-war in the Pacific Fleet from 1946, and was transferred to the reserves in 1957 with the rank of lieutenant colonel.

In this photograph of Maj Petr Sgibnev, taken at Vaenga-1 in the spring of 1943, he is wearing two Order of the Red Banner badges on his tunic but no HSU star. Sgibnev had received the Soviet Union's highest award for bravery in combat in October 1942. Note the Hurricane IIC armed with four 20 mm Hispano cannon parked in the background. The Northern Fleet Air Force had received a small number of these heavily armed aircraft in March 1943

On 11 November 1942 fellow Hurricane ace Aleksey Dizhevskiy claimed his last victory when he reported shooting down a Ju 88, and later that month he was given command of 78th IAP's 2nd Squadron. In May 1943 he became CO of the Northern Fleet Air Force's 27th IAP, where he remained until the end of combat operations in this theatre. Dizhevskiy transferred to the Pacific fleet in 1944, and in 1957 to the reserve with the rank of colonel.

Seven-victory Hurricane ace Lt Col Aleksey Dizhevskiy, CO of 27th IAP, is seen here at far left in the regimental command post during the summer of 1943

Vasiliy Doroshin was also CO of a 78th IAP squadron by November 1942, and he claimed his last victory (a Ju 88) on 21 February 1943. He failed to return from a sortie in Hurricane JS259 on 23 June that same year, one account of his death noting 'there were no encounters with enemy aircraft during the sortie, and the area around the target was covered by anti-aircraft artillery fire. On the way back at low level his radiator and propeller hit the water. The pilot made a technical error when entering low-level flight, for he got caught in the slipstream of an Il-2. His propeller hit the water and the aircraft crashed and sank'.

Doroshin had logged 437 sorties, 11 of them at night, by the time he was killed. Of his 600 flying hours, 348 were in the Hurricane.

Kurzenkov's Last Battle

Despite his past misdemeanours, Guards Capt Sergey Kurzenkov became deputy CO of 78th IAP in November 1942. He would not survive in this role for long, however.

Northern Fleet pilots often took off individually to attack enemy airfields under the cover of darkness, aircraft being sent aloft with short intervals between each machine. These sorties, however, proved to be as ineffective as they were difficult and dangerous to fly. Bombs were often dropped wide of the target in the face of heavy anti-aircraft fire. Flying in all-enveloping darkness, pilots were unable to observe the results of their attacks. And although flak and nightfighters posed a threat to the Soviet crews, their biggest enemy was the rapidly changing polar weather. In December 1942 alone, four aircraft (a Pe-2 bomber, a USB biplane, a Hurricane and a LaGG-3) were lost to bad weather conditions and six airmen died. Apart from that, it was not uncommon for aircraft to be targeted by 'friendly' anti-aircraft batteries while returning from a sortie as gun crews would fire furiously at any aircraft flying into their sector.

Kurzenkov took off in his heavily laden Hurricane on the evening of 28 February 1943 for his seventh nocturnal sortie. His mission was to attack an enemy airfield – he was not only an ace but also a capable ground attack pilot. Indeed, Kurzenkov had already destroyed a Ju 88 in a revetment and an adjacent building that provided accommodation for up to 12 personnel. Now, flying alone at an altitude of around 1500 m (5000 ft), Kurzenkov reached the target and dropped two 50 kg (110 lb)

Six-victory Hurricane ace Vasiliy Doroshin was born in 1921 to a peasant family in the Leningrad region. In 1939 he entered Chuguev Military Aviation School and began his service with 72nd SAP in October 1940 as a junior pilot flying I-153 fighters. Doroshin converted to Hurricanes in the winter of 1941-42 as a member of 2nd GKAP

bombs from a shallow dive. Enemy artillery threw up a fierce anti-aircraft barrage and Kurzenkov felt shrapnel hit both the engine of his fighter and his left leg as he pulled out of his dive. Fearing that his engine might stop at any moment, Kurzenkov decided not to head for the sea but instead steered a straight course for home, despite this route taking him over enemy-held territory.

There were designated 'air corridors' over Soviet territory, and any aircraft flying outside them was regarded as hostile. But losing blood and nursing a badly damaged aircraft, Kurzenkov had no choice but to ignore the 'air corridors', as having crossed the frontline, he had to take the shortest route back to his own airfield before he passed out. Within minutes of entering Soviet airspace his Hurricane, AM356, was caught in searchlights and he was immediately targeted by intense anti-aircraft fire. Unable to fly the last few kilometres back to base, Kurzenkov was forced to bail out from a height of just 80 m (260 ft). To make matters worse, his parachute had been damaged when the Hurricane was hit by shrapnel, and it did little to retard his fall. Luckily for him, Kurzenkov landed on the side of a steep hill that was covered by deep snow, allowing him to survive the heavy impact.

A soldier from the airfield service battalion stumbled across the seriously wounded pilot, who had lost consciousness. Sergey Kurzenkov underwent two surgical procedures and his damaged right kidney was removed. After a lengthy convalescence, he spent the rest of his military career on administrative duties. Kurzenkov was subsequently awarded the title of HSU by a state decree dated 24 July 1943. In less than 18 months of fighting Sergey Kurzenkov had flown 197 operational sorties (one source puts the figure at 209), logged 214 flying hours and participated in 20 aerial battles. He was transferred to the reserves with the rank of colonel in August 1950 and died on 18 November 1981.

As the polar nights shortened in 1943, combat activity in the skies above Murmansk intensified as the number of aircraft on either side increased. But with many pilots reporting the simultaneous destruction of enemy aircraft, it is now virtually impossible to determine who the victors really were.

A Hurricane IIB is prepared for a night mission during early 1943. Such sorties, which targeted enemy airfields, proved difficult to fly because of poor weather conditions – night flights were only performed by a small number of highly experienced pilots. These missions were, in the main, largely ineffective

BATTLES OVER THE OCEAN

Northern Fleet Air Force units continued to soldier on with their Hurricanes in the early months of 1943. Pilots were flying aircraft that were much the same as the Hawker fighters that had first seen service with the RAF back in 1938, yet they were now having to contend with a formidable new generation of enemy fighters. These included the latest variants of the Messerschmitt Bf 109, the G-2/6 series, as well as the Focke-Wulf Fw 190.

It might seem almost unthinkable that Soviet pilots could still shoot down enough enemy aircraft while flying such obsolete fighters in 1943 to earn themselves the title of ace. However, as late as 20 July that year, Hurricane ace Jr Lt Aleksey Pilipenko was still regularly engaging the Luftwaffe in the British machine. Addressing a conference of pilots from 27th and 78th IAPs, he listed the pitfalls and extolled the virtues of an aircraft that he had plenty of combat experience in;

'The design of the Hurricane is an obsolete one dating back to 1934. It is a large fighter and has a thick wing. It can be detected easily in the air, is weak in the vertical fight, slow to gain speed and quick to lose it. The engine cuts out in a dive and you have to close the throttle and then open it again smoothly to restore power. On the positive side, it has excellent armament and good manoeuvrability, which can be used to advantage in dogfights with enemy aircraft in conjunction with faster types like the Yak-1 and the Airacobra.'

This frank assessment suggests that even in 1943 the Hurricane was still capable of giving a good account of itself when used in coordination with higher performance fighters.

That year the Northern Fleet Air Force command found itself with no ground attack aircraft at its disposal at a time when it was called upon to disrupt the enemy's coastal supply convoys. Hurricanes of 78th IAP were therefore hastily equipped with underwing bomb racks and the first attack on German shipping attempted on 17 February. The aircraft were re-deployed from Vaenga-1 to Zubovka airfield under the command of Hurricane ace Capt Aleksey Dizhevskiy so as to bring them within closer range of enemy vessels. The fighters were not to be there for very long, however.

The deployment got off to a bad start when one of the aircraft in-bound from Vaenga-1 was shot down by two Bf 109s, Sgt V P Chukov, flying Hurricane DR356, being attacked while making his landing approach. A few hours later the airfield was targeted by Bf 110 fighter-bombers, escorted by Bf 109s. By then 78th IAP had already flown several sorties from Zubovka, which lacked any protection for aircraft, as well as inadequate flak defences. Accordingly, the Hurricane pilots were anxious to return to Vaenga-1.

Aleksey Pilipenko, born the son of a clerk in 1912 in the Rostov region, entered Eysk Naval Aviation School in 1940 and graduated two years later. Posted to 78th IAP, Northern Fleet Air Force, he scored the first of his six Hurricane victories on 2 June 1942. Pilipenko was twice awarded the Order of the Red Banner prior to being killed in action on 20 July 1943

Sustained attacks on enemy shipping began at the end of May when several successful raids on individual vessels were made by groups of six to eight aircraft. On 1 June Hurricanes of 78th IAP began joint operations with Il-2s of 46th ShAP, which had become part of the Northern Fleet Air Force in March. For the next three months the regiment had been undergoing combat training prior to it being declared operationally capable.

Il-2 ground attack aircraft of 46th ShAP, Northern Fleet Air Force, fly over the polar tundra. 78th IAP Hurricanes were the first fighters to escort these aircraft on offensive missions

With its relatively low cruising speed, the Hurricane was well suited to the job of escorting the ground attack aircraft. And the Northern Fleet Air Force command considered that these mixed groups would have enough combined firepower to protect themselves against enemy fighters.

The first joint operation, conducted on 1 June, followed shortly after a Soviet reconnaissance aircraft had detected a German convoy nearing port. At 0100 hrs four Il-2s led by Capt Aleksey Mazurenko took off to attack the vessels, escorted by eight Hurricanes. Mazurenko was the senior flying instructor of Soviet ground attack aviation at this time, and he had been posted to the Northern Fleet to train Il-2 pilots in how to target ships at sea. He ended the war a twice HSU with a score of eight ships sunk and 22 shared destroyed. Although Mazurenko attacked the vessels, for pilots of 46th ShAP this was just a familiarisation sortie.

A few days later the mixed group of Il-2s and Hurricanes was redeployed northeast to the frontline airfield at Pummanki, on the Sredniy peninsula, for more shipping attacks. There, they were just 15-17 km (9-11 miles) from the Red Army's main line of defence, and only 25 km (16 miles) from the German naval base at Liinakhamari, in Petsamo bay. But this move also brought the Soviet aircraft closer to the enemy airfield at Luostari, home of JG 5 *Eismeer*.

This mixed group soon became a thorn in the side of the Germans, with the exploits of Hurricane ace and 78th IAP squadron commander Capt Vasiliy Adonkin being particularly noteworthy during this period. A respected and popular pilot who had fought as a member of the Northern Fleet Air Force since the start of the war, Adonkin had been one of the first Soviet aviators presented with the Order of the Red Banner, on 14 July 1941, for an action in which he engaged German bombers while flying an I-153. Three Ju 88s were reported to have been shot down, but their loss remains unconfirmed. Adonkin received his second Order of the Red Banner on 2 June 1942 after

It was believed that the UB 12.7 mm defensive machine guns of the Il-2, combined with the weapons of the escorting Hurricanes, would provide a strong enough defence against opposing Bf 109s. In practice, however, this concept quickly proved to be fatally flawed

recording his fifth victory (flying an I-16) while serving as a squadron commander with 27th IAP.

Vasiliy Adonkin was born the son of a clerk in 1918 in the Belgorod region. In 1937, after his first year in the Pedagogical Institute, he entered Eysk Naval Aviation School and, after graduation in 1940, was posted to the Northern Fleet Air Force. When the war began he was flying the I-153, and he subsequently converted to the I-16. Adonkin started flying Hurricanes in March 1943, by which time he had already claimed seven kills. On 12 June 1943 he shot down the first of five aerial victories he would achieve in the Hurricane. On 22 January 1944 Adonkin was awarded the title of HSU, and he also received the Order of the Red Banner three times. He failed to return from a combat mission on 17 March 1944

When his regiment was re-equipped with Hurricanes at the end of March 1943, Adonkin was one of the first pilots to convert. He was subsequently appointed deputy commander of 27th IAP, and would probably have progressed further but for his addiction to alcohol, which resulted in his demotion and transfer to 78th IAP. Adonkin was sent to Pummanki airfield as a squadron CO, and by this time he had been credited with six victories over Bf 109s, plus a further seven shared kills. Given the job of escorting Il-2 ground attack aircraft, Adonkin soon provided further confirmation of his prowess as a fighter pilot by claiming two enemy aircraft shot down on 12 June.

Flying a night mission, four Il-2s, led by Capt Mazurenko, had attacked enemy shipping near Lille Ekkerey Island. The *Shturmoviks* were escorted by eight Hurricanes, with Capt Adonkin in the lead fighter. According to pilots' reports, the raid inflicted heavy losses on the enemy – a 1500-ton transport and two 120-ton launches were sunk and fires started on the quayside. The defending fighters managed to intercept the mixed group of attack aircraft as they were leaving the target area. The Hurricanes engaged two Bf 110s and six Bf 109s in combat, and according to the Soviet pilots, shot down four enemy fighters – two of each type. Adonkin claimed a Bf 109 and a Bf 110 for his seventh and eighth victories. Two young pilots recorded their first kills during this

Capt Adonkin of 78th IAP poses with his Hurricane IIB on 20 June 1943. He would claim five victories with the British fighter to add to the seven he scored flying I-153s and I-16s in 1941-42

battle, Jr Lts Maslennikov and Nour reportedly downing a Bf 109 and a Bf 110 respectively, but their claims are unconfirmed. Low cloud and poor visibility aided the safe return of the Soviet formation without loss.

The shipping strikes did not continue to go unpunished, however. That same evening nine Ju 87s, escorted by 11 Bf 109s, raided Pummanki and three Hurricanes sustained slight damage. From that day onwards the airfield was subjected to systematic air attacks and shelling by Wehrmacht artillery batteries on the opposite bank of the Sredniy peninsula. The Soviet ground attack aircraft also suffered at the hands of Luftwaffe fighters. Indeed, the records of JG 5 show that during the next sortie mounted by the Il-2s and Hurricanes, on 13 June, Bf 109s downed a *Shturmovik* and damaged Hurricane BD931. The pilot of the latter machine, Jr Lt Andrey Nikolayev, managed to nurse his damaged aircraft as far as the Rybachiy peninsula, where he made an emergency landing that left him injured and the fighter destroyed.

These losses prompted the use of faster P-39s and Yak-1s as part of the attack group, their task being to provide close escort for the Hurricanes and Il-2s in an attempt to deter the Bf 109s from targeting the Soviet aircraft. In practice, it proved difficult for the escort fighters to properly coordinate their efforts with the ground attack aircraft. Often, en route to the target, the P-39s and Yak-1s would leave the aircraft they were supposed to be escorting to engage Luftwaffe fighters, thus exposing the Il-2s and Hurricanes to attack from other Bf 109s. And Yak-1 pilots were also reluctant to stay and fight with enemy fighters due to the aircraft's small fuel reserves. As a result, they frequently broke away from their charges, leaving the Il-2s and Hurricanes without cover.

It was not long before the anti-shipping sorties boiled over into fully-fledged aerial battles. One of the first major operations against an enemy convoy was conducted on 19 June. That some day Adonkin claimed another victory whilst leading eight Hurricanes that were accompanying four Il-2s – six Yak-1s and eight P-39s provided the fighter escort. At 0300 hrs the attack aircraft swept in from 400 m (1300 ft) to engage the enemy convoy. Comprising three transports, five patrol boats and two minesweepers, it was approaching its home port of Liinakhamari with an escort of 13 Bf 109s and four Bf 110s circling overhead.

The Soviet aircraft were still eight kilometres (five miles) from the target when they were intercepted by a large force of enemy fighters. Some of the Messerschmitts engaged the Hurricanes, which in turn became separated from the Il-2s. The latter were left unprotected, as the 20 Yak-1s from 20th IAP that should have been providing a fighter escort were still at high altitude. They eventually arrived over the convoy just as the battle was ending. By then the Il-2s had managed to evade the fighters and fight their way to the ships. Making a single pass, the *Shturmoviks* strafed, rocketed and bombed the vessels from an altitude of 200 m (650 ft).

Fighting for their survival, the Hurricane pilots engaged in a fierce battle with the opposing fighters, which soon gained the upper hand. No fewer than five Hurricanes (AM274, KX144, KX404, KX488 and KX730) were shot down into the sea, resulting in the deaths of Jr Lts Vasiliy Nazarov (a flight commander), Petr Gaplikov and Nikolai Starosvetskiy. Lts Yuriy Maslennikov and Fyodor Kochanov bailed out of their burning aircraft and were quickly rescued from the water by launches. Two more damaged Hurricanes made emergency landings at Pummanki, as did an Il-2, leaving the remaining attack aircraft (escorted by Yak-1s and P-39s) to fly back to Vaenga-1. Apart from Adonkin, fellow Hurricane pilots Lts Z V Bulat (his third victory), F M Kochanov (first victory) and V G Mitrofanov (second victory) from his squadron each claimed a Bf 109 destroyed.

June 1943 also saw another 78th IAP pilot become a Hurricane ace when, on the 5th, flight commander Jr Lt Aleksey Pilipenko recorded his fifth victory while covering a convoy of ships in the Gulf of Motovsk. Such duties also fell to the Northern Fleet fighter pilots, in addition to mounting attacks on enemy shipping. Ensuring the safety of Soviet convoys was a critical mission since the troops defending the peninsulas of Rybachiy and Sredniy depended on being re-supplied by sea.

FIGHTING OVER THE GULF OF MOTOVSK

Fighters constantly patrolled the Gulf of Motovsk during this period too, on the alert for marauding Bf 109s and Fw 190s attempting to attack Soviet ships. And when enemy aircraft were encountered, the Northern Fleet pilots were often at a disadvantage because the German machines usually sortied in numerically superior formations. This meant that despite their best efforts, the Soviet fighters could not prevent Luftwaffe aircraft from attacking shipping. The proximity of enemy airfields also gave JG 5 more time in the target area, with pilots from the unit operating over friendly territory for the first time in two years. No longer worried about being captured should they have to bail out, they pressed home their attacks over the Gulf of Motovsk with previously unseen ferocity during June 1943. This was demonstrated by the fact that 18 Hurricanes were shot down in battles over the supply convoys during the course of the month, resulting in the loss of eight pilots.

On 5 June, during one of the bloodiest battles of the campaign, Jr Lt Aleksey Pilipenko became a Hurricane ace. Many of the details pertaining to the fighting on this date are, however, obscure, with the limited archival documentation available making it impossible to provide an exact account of the actions of each participant. What is known is that 50 fighters were ordered by Northern Fleet Air Force command to cover a single barge carrying ten new 122 mm field guns and 60 artillerymen. It was being towed by a tug and accompanied by four Maritime Defence launches. Hurricanes comprised the main element of the airborne escort, with 20 from 78th IAP and 16 from 27th IAP.

Between 0445 hrs and 0705 hrs, two major aerial battles were fought. In the first, Hurricanes from 78th IAP attempted to fend off two formations of Bf 109s and Fw 190s. Soviet sources put the total number of German fighters involved at 20. 78th IAP quickly lost four Hurricanes, Jr Lts N T Starosvetskiy and V A Kukibniy bailing out of their burning aircraft, while the other two pilots, Jr Lts N I Kirillov and N A Kravchenko, were able to make emergency landings on the Rybachiy peninsula. Kravchenko's aircraft was then strafed by a Messerschmitt and set on fire, seriously wounding the pilot.

Thirty minutes later there was another battle when 12 Hurricanes from 27th and 78th IAPs, escorted by P-39s from 255th IAP, were

Commander of the 1st Squadron of 78th IAP, Snr Lt A E Tulskiy scored his first aerial victory on 18 June 1942 when he shot down a Ju 87 by firing four rocket projectiles at it from his I-15bis fighter. In 1943, following his regiment's switch to the Hurricane, Tulskiy reported shooting down three Bf 109Gs

attacked by 12 Bf 109s and eight Fw 190s, split into two groups. The Focke-Wulfs made a low-level attack on the convoy while the Bf 109s targeted the escorting fighters. According to Soviet pilot reports, the Germans lost a combined total of seven Bf 109s and one Fw 190 in these two encounters, with a further two described as probables. Snr Lt A E Tulskiy (his second victory), Kukibniy (second), Kravchenko (second), Pilipenko (fifth), Jr Lt N G Kashcheev (second) and Snr Sgts B G Ermolin (first) and N I Kirillov (first) each claimed to have shot down a Bf 109. Capt A A Krasilnikov of 27th IAP also claimed his first kill, an Fw 190. German sources, however, list only one loss over the Gulf of Motovsk that day – Bf 109 Wk-Nr. 7480 of 9./JG 5, killing pilot Leutnant Helmut Steinle. In view of the multiplicity of claims, it is impossible to determine which of the Soviet pilots downed this aircraft.

Soviet losses, however, were far greater. Apart from the four 78th IAP Hurricanes already mentioned, five more were lost in the second battle, resulting in the deaths of Capt V A Ageychev and Jr Lt P M Savitskiy. Ageychev was a squadron commander and one of the regiment's most experienced pilots with 190 sorties and four kills to his credit. Savitskiy had claimed one victory.

The cargo, so vital to the defenders of Rybachiy and Sredniy, was safely delivered, although the cost had been high – nine Hurricanes were shot down (BW959, BW984, HW233, JS351, KX106, KX491, KX526, Z2461 and Z5134) and two pilots killed.

Pilipenko had joined 78th IAP's 3rd Squadron at the end of June following the death of fellow Hurricane ace Capt Vasiliy Doroshin. However, the Northern Fleet ace was not to command the unit for long, for he too failed to return from a sortie on the night of 20-21 July. At 2240 hrs Pilipenko had led six Hurricanes aloft to provide close escort for seven Il-2s ordered to attack enemy shipping. Further cover was provided by seven P-39s of 255th IAP. Whilst returning from the target area, the mixed formation was intercepted by 12 Bf 109s. Three Hurricanes were shot down, killing Pilipenko and Jr Lts Sergey Volkov and Ivan Shakhov. This was the ace's 221st operational sortie, and he had logged a total of 262 flying hours prior to his death. His subordinates Volkov and Shakhov had just 81 hrs and 14 hrs, respectively.

In the aftermath of these losses, an official document stated that 'the lack of coordination between the groups of aircraft in combat was demonstrated by the way the faster fighters did not cover the Hurricanes as they broke off combat. The close escort group, which had engaged a superior force of enemy aircraft, could not disengage. The leading groups of Airacobra and Il-2 aircraft, instead of assisting the Hurricanes, retreated by themselves'. In other words, the 78th IAP pilots were abandoned by their comrades to be torn to pieces by a superior force of enemy aircraft.

Aleksey Pilipenko had died believing that the Hurricane could be successful, provided it was allowed to fight in conjunction with higher

performance fighters, although this clearly did not always happen. He was just 21 when killed, and had achieved his first victory while flying a Hurricane on 2 June 1942 when he shot down a Ju 87 dive-bombing the port of Murmansk. By the time he claimed his second success, Pilipenko had been promoted to senior sergeant and made CO of a squadron. By the end of 1942 he was considered one of the most experienced pilots in 78th IAP, and he often shared that experience with other pilots at their conferences. He was twice awarded the Order of the Red Banner. When 27th IAP converted to the Hurricane Pilipenko offered to help the regiment's pilots become familiar with their new equipment. He recorded his sixth victory, over a Bf 109, during his final battle, and was posthumously promoted to senior lieutenant.

Snr Lt V I Zorin, a 27th IAP squadron commander, briefs his pilots for their next Hurricane mission shortly after the unit swapped its elderly I-15bis biplanes for the British fighter in the spring of 1943

Fellow Hurricane ace Capt Vasiliy Adonkin had been awarded his third Order of the Red Banner just prior to Pilipenko's death. In late July 1943 Adonkin was put forward for the title of HSU, although he did not receive it for a further six months. The official recommendation for the award noted that 'during his period of combat activity, Comrade Adonkin flew 365 combat sorties, logged 372 flying hours and has fought in 42 air battles, during which he has destroyed ten enemy aircraft. He made 31 successful attacks on enemy ground troops, other targets and small enemy vessels. He also carried out bombing raids, followed by ground attacks on paratroops landing in the area around

Capt Vasiliy Adonkin of 78th IAP poses with his Hurricane at Pummanki airfield prior to flying an escort mission for Il-2s targeting German shipping in the Barents Sea in the summer of 1943

Malaya Volokovaya Bay, and attacked a large number of enemy troops close to the River Zapadnaya Litsa. In the period between 1 June and 6 July 1943, Comrade Adonkin commanded seven attacks on small enemy vessels, during which two motorboats were sunk, and three motorboats and one transport vessel, displacing up to 1500 tons, as well as a single patrol boat, were set on fire'.

Adonkin scored his last Hurricane victory with 78th IAP on 22 August. On that day the Northern Fleet ace led a mixed group of six Hurricanes and four I-16s tasked with strafing enemy aircraft at a frontline airfield on the shores of Varanger Fjord. Having taken off before dawn, the Soviet fighters managed to hit the target accurately, despite difficult weather conditions. The pilots observed one aircraft on fire before engaging about ten Bf 109s. After they had all returned from their sortie the Northern Fleet pilots reported shooting down five enemy aircraft, although this tally was unconfirmed. The following pilots each claimed a Bf 109 – Vasiliy Adonkin (his 11th victory according to the journals of enemy aircraft destroyed), Capt Vasiliy Pronchenko (his fifth victory, making him a Hurricane ace) and Snr Lts Ivan Popovich (second), Semyon Podyachev (second) and Nour (fourth).

Like Pronchenko, Adonkin's victory took his total of Hurricane kills to five. Shortly thereafter he was transferred to 255th IAP and appointed aide to the regimental commander in charge of flying training. He also converted to the P-39. On 22 January 1944 Adonkin was awarded the title of HSU by order of the Presidium of the Supreme Soviet. During the first three months of 1944 he shot down two more Bf 109s, but on 17 March he failed to return from a sortie. Adonkin had taken off on his 370th operational mission to escort torpedo bombers attacking a large convoy of enemy ships. The following account by a 255th IAP pilot was noted in the official combat report;

'We ran into a heavy snow shower en route to the target. The leader of the group of escort fighters, Guards Capt Vasiliy Adonkin, gained height to fly over the snowstorm, together with his wingman, Jr Lt Smirnov, who was able to return despite his aircraft being seriously iced up. Guards Capt Adonkin continued to fly on after his aircraft became iced up and he is presumed to have crashed near the Rybachiy Peninsula.'

This heavily retouched photograph features Hurricane IIB Z3768 adorned with the legend 'For the VKPb'. It was regularly flown by eight-victory ace Capt Dmitriy Amosov of 78th IAP, Northern Fleet Air Force, in 1941-42

A little over a month later, on 10 May 1944, fellow 255th IAP Northern Fleet Hurricane ace and squadron commander Dmitriy Amosov was also killed during the course of what would have been his 321st combat sortie. Official records show that he had destroyed eight enemy aircraft, six on them in the Hurricane. Like Adonkin, he had first flown with 27th SAP of the Northern Fleet Air Force in the far north in the early days of the war. He shot down his first aircraft on 23 August 1941 while flying an I-153. German records, incidentally, confirm the loss of Bf 109E-3 Wk-Nr. 1118 during this engagement, together with its pilot, Leutnant Hans Malkuch. Later that same day Jr Lt Amosov was awarded the Order of the Red Banner.

After converting to the Hurricane with 78th IAP, he increased his score by two more kills. As a flight commander, Amosov became one of the first pilots to achieve success with the Hurricane in the newly formed unit when, on 15 December 1941, he reported shooting down his third enemy aircraft, which remained unconfirmed. Amosov was transferred to 2nd GKAP in March 1942, where he served as acting deputy squadron commander. On 4 April he recorded his fifth victory when he joined two other Northern Fleet aces, Aleksander Kovalenko and Sergey Kurzenkov, in intercepting a pair of Bf 109Es over the frontline. The German fighters were pursuing Pe-2 fighter-bombers when the three Hurricanes attacked the Messerschmitts head-on, using their machine guns and RS-82 rockets. According to the pilots' reports, the Bf 109s quickly turned round and headed back to the west trailing smoke and losing altitude. German sources indicate that one pilot, Unteroffizier Artur Mendl, suffered head wounds during this battle with the Hurricanes.

It was on 30 May that Amosov reported his sixth victory. He was flying one of six Hurricanes that engaged four Bf 109s over the Allied convoy PQ-16 as it entered the Kola Gulf, the official combat report for the action stating;

'Our pilots sighted two Me 110s and five Me 109s in the area they were patrolling at an altitude of 1000 m and engaged them in combat. Snr Lt Amosov opened fire with four bursts from behind an Me 109 at a range of 200-150 m and drove it into the water.'

This is, however, unconfirmed. Amosov failed to spot an approaching enemy aircraft and came under fire himself. He was severely wounded and managed to ditch in the sea, being rescued by sailors. Following a lengthy spell in hospital, the Northern Fleet ace was sent on a course to improve his skills as a squadron commander. Earlier, on 23 July 1942, Amosov had been awarded his second Order of the Red Banner. Upon his return to combat in May 1943 he led a squadron within 27th IAP, which at that time was undergoing combat training on the Hurricane. Using his experience, Amosov was able to facilitate that process.

Following a break of more than a year, the Northern Fleet ace recorded his seventh victory on 28 August 1943. It was also his fifth with the Hurricane. His victim was probably Bf 109G-2 Wk-Nr. 10844, from which Feldwebel Hans Enderle managed to bail out. Amosov had been leading a group of Hurricanes which, together with Il-2s, had taken off to attack an enemy airfield. Although each Hurricane was carrying a FAB-50 bomb under its fuselage, Amosov's pilots had been ordered to escort the ground attack aircraft, despite the presence of other Hurricanes, Yak-1s and P-39s.

As the raiders were approaching their target Bf 109s appeared, one of which attempted to attack an Il-2 from behind. Amosov poured two long bursts of machine gun fire into the fighter, which immediately burst into flames, forcing the pilot to bail out. Although the escort group pilots were unable to confirm this victory, it was verified by several of the Il-2 pilots. According to Amosov's combat report, he used 62 20 mm ShVAK shells and 60 12.7 mm large calibre rounds to destroy the Bf 109G-2.

Dmitriy Amosov was born in 1915 to a peasant family living in the Rostov region. He entered Eysk Naval Aviation School in 1939, and at the end of the following year Amosov was posted to the Northern Fleet Air Force. Serving as an I-153 pilot with 72th SAP at the beginning of the war, Amosov converted to the Hurricane in October 1941 with newly formed 78th IAP. By that time he had already scored two aerial victories, and added the first of five as a Hurricane pilot on 15 December 1941. In May 1943 Amosov became a squadron commander with 27th IAP, Northern Fleet Air Force. He was killed in action on 10 May 1944 while flying a P-39 with 225th IAP, having by then claimed eight victories. Amosov was twice awarded the Order of the Red Banner

Snr Lt Ivan Edush began his combat career in 1943 flying Hurricanes with 27th IAP. He scored two aerial victories with the type prior to the regiment converting to the P-40. The latter type was eventually replaced by the P-39, and Edush was flying an Airacobra when he was shot down and killed on 12 October 1944. He had accounted for five enemy aircraft prior to his demise

The air battle did not end there, however, as during the second approach to the target more Bf 109s attempted to break through the escorting fighters in an effort to reach the Il-2s, but they were frustrated. The defence of the *Shturmoviks* cost three Hurricanes and a Yak-1, and two pilots killed. One of the downed Hurricanes came from Amosov's group, its pilot, Jr Lt T F Chistov, performing an emergency landing near the enemy airfield. He managed to return to his base two days later.

Reorganisation

In October 1943 there was a reorganisation intended to improve training efficiency between the Hurricane-equipped 27th IAP and 255th IAP. As the most proficient in the former unit, Amosov's squadron was transferred to 255th to convert to the P-39. A squadron from the latter regiment, which had started transitioning to the P-40, was in turn transferred to the 27th. As a result, Dmitriy Amosov, now holding the rank of captain, started to train for operations on another type of fighter in another regiment. He quickly earned the respect of his new colleagues and continued to fly the Airacobra, scoring his eighth, and final, victory on 7 April 1944. A month later, while returning from a sortie, and witnessed by his regimental colleagues, Amosov crashed into the water and was killed.

His death followed a torpedo attack on a German convoy, the escorting fighter pilots strafing the decks of the enemy ships with their machine guns for two or three minutes in response to heavy anti-aircraft fire. On the return flight a trail of white smoke was visible behind the leader's aircraft, and a few minutes later the pilots in the group heard the call 'It's me, Amosov. I can't see'. As the white smoke turned to black his fellow pilots radioed directions to him, but for some unknown reason Amosov failed to gain height, thus preventing him from safely bailing out of his P-39 – perhaps he preferred a quick death to capture by the enemy. Putting his aircraft into a steep dive, Amosov shouted his final order over the radio – 'Bring the torpedo-bombers home'. His Airacobra, smoking heavily, crashed into the water at high speed and plunged beneath the waves.

Compared with the heroic and dramatic exploits of Vasiliy Adonkin and Dmitriy Amosov, those of fellow Hurricane ace Capt Vasiliy Pronchenko seem less impressive. Yet he not only fought in, and survived, the bloody polar battles, but also recorded the destruction of five enemy aircraft. Pronchenko 'made ace' on 22 August 1943 – the same day that Vasiliy Adonkin recorded his fifth individual victory in the Hurricane. And like the latter, the military career of Vasiliy Pronchenko developed in a way that was far from straightforward.

Joining the Northern Fleet as a lieutenant in April 1942 (the most difficult period of the air war in this theatre), Pronchenko had previously spent three years as a flying instructor at an aviation college prior to becoming a pilot in 2nd GKAP. He scored his first victory on 30 May 1942, over a Bf 109, his combat report stating that Pronchenko was flying one of six Hurricanes that had taken off to intercept enemy aircraft over the entrance to Kola Bay. Here, they engaged five Bf 109s and two Bf 110s, and in the ensuing battle the Northern Fleet pilots claimed to have destroyed two single-seat fighters, as well as a probable, but this

Five-victory Hurricane ace Vasiliy Pronchenko was born in 1918 to a peasant family in the Chernigov region. Entering Eysk Naval Aviation School in 1937, he became a flying instructor upon graduation. In March 1942 Pronchenko was posted to 2nd GKAP of the Northern Fleet Air Force, and he claimed his first aerial victory on 30 May that same year. At war's end Pronchenko was serving as adjutant of 54th SAP, White Sea Flotilla Air Force

is unconfirmed. Two Hurricanes were lost in return. The official report detailing Vasiliy Pronchenko's first kill read as follows;

'He gave the Me 109 two bursts of fire from a distance of 20-150 m, after which the enemy aircraft turned onto its wing and went down, crashing into the water. Lt Pronchenko was slightly injured.'

As it happened, the leg wound inflicted on the future ace represented a lucky escape for the Northern Fleet pilot, as 80 bullet holes were counted in his aircraft upon his return to base.

A little more than two weeks later, on 18 June, Pronchenko reported shooting down his second victim, a Ju 87. On this occasion he was flying in a group of five Hurricanes, led by Kurzenkov, that attacked a large formation of dive-bombers. Pronchenko made two attacks on one of them, initially from below and behind from a range of 150 m and then from below and to port from 50-70 m. As he reported later, Pronchenko could see 'the impact of my fire hitting the Ju 87's fuselage behind the cockpit'. The aircraft crashed ten kilometres [six miles] southwest of Murmansk. Although this kill remained unconfirmed, it nevertheless made a favourable impression on Pronchenko's regimental superiors, for in early June he was promoted and made a flight commander.

As previously noted, Northern Fleet fighter operations were restricted during the second half of 1942 by the lack of serviceable equipment. It was not, therefore, until the following year that Pronchenko was able to continue making a name for himself. The 19 March 1943 combat report states that Hurricanes took off to intercept a Ju 88, and that Pronchenko 'attacked the bomber at an altitude of 4500 m [14,625 ft]. The aircraft subsequently crashed near Lake Kyadel-Yavr'. This is not confirmed.

After claiming his third kill Pronchenko received his first decoration, the Order of the Red Banner. He was promoted again and made a deputy squadron commander in 78th IAP. Pronchenko reported his fourth victory on 13 June, claiming to have downed a Bf 110 while he was escorting Il-2s attacking enemy shipping. This kill is also unconfirmed. By November, when Pronchenko had claimed five victories, he was also serving as regimental navigation officer. Six months later, however, he was removed from this post, demoted and transferred to 54th SAP of the Belarussian Flotilla. He remained there until the end of the war, by which point he was serving as an adjutant. In 1951 Pronchenko was transferred to the reserves.

This Northern Fleet Air Force Hurricane IIA was modified for night operations through the fitment of an anti-glare shield over the engine exhausts

The career of fellow Hurricane ace Vasiliy Strelnikov was almost a mirror image of Pronchenko's. He too would claim five kills as a Hurricane pilot, but his early service was marked by a strange incident, the details of which were subsequently circulated outside the Northern Fleet. The *Bulletin of Navy Air Force Combat Losses* related combat experiences of naval pilots fighting the Germans. In April 1943 Strelnikov was a virtually unknown senior sergeant whose name was about to become widely reported for all the wrong reasons in the pages of the *Bulletin*.

On 13 April four 78th IAP Hurricanes, led by Snr Lt Veryovkin, took off together with two Kittyhawks from 2nd GKAB. Strelnikov and Veryovkin were flying the leading pair of Hurricanes, and they sighted five Bf 109s approaching from out of the sun. Strelnikov failed to warn Veryovkin because he assumed that the element leader could see them too. This carelessness was to cost the regiment dearly, as the Messerschmitt pilots were able to position themselves on the Hurricanes' tails and attack them. Strelnikov attempted to counter an attack by a pair of Bf 109s, and again he failed to warn his leader of the danger. Moments later Strelnikov was shot down by another pair of enemy aircraft. His wingman, Sgt Ilya Kostenyuk, was also attacked, but his opponents were poor shots and missed their target. Having dodged the attack, he dived away not only from the Messerschmitts but also from his own flight. However, when he saw Strelnikov bailing out of his stricken aircraft, Kostenyuk covered his landing before returning to base.

Strelnikov had struggled to escape the cockpit of his aircraft, which had burst into flames when enemy fire had holed the forward fuel tank behind the instrument panel. The escaping fuel caught fire and Strelnikov suffered burns to his face and neck. His face was also scratched by the strap of his parachute when he finally jumped free, and he had lost his boots as he tumbled through the air. Strelnikov landed bare-footed and had to walk several kilometres through the snow. He subsequently spent 20 days in hospital.

Squadronmate Sgt Aleksander Besputko had not been so lucky. Suffering fatal wounds when his aircraft (JS365) was hit by enemy fire, he was still strapped into his blazing Hurricane when it dived away and exploded upon hitting the ground. Snr Lt Mikhail Veryovkin suffered serious damage to his aircraft too, yet despite the failure of its engine he was able to make a deadstick landing back at base. Even 2nd GKAB incurred a solitary loss when the Kittyhawk of Guards Snr Lt Nikolai Zapalenov was shot down in poor visibility, the pilot being forced to bail out of his burning aircraft.

The *Bulletin's* verdict on the principal cause of these losses was the 'carelessness and complete lack of good judgment from leaders, and also from the pilots within groups and pairs'. The actions of Snr Sgt Strelnikov in particular were described as 'criminal inactivity'. Fortunately for Vasiliy Strelnikov, the Northern Fleet Air Force command considered it unnecessary to bring him before a military tribunal, even though other combat pilots had been sent to punishment battalions for lesser offences.

This ill-fated mission had been Strelnikov's 28th operational sortie, and he had just 42 flying hours in combat to his name at the time. In fact all of his operational flying over the past three-and-a-half months had been in the Hurricane. Strelnikov had been a flight commander since January, and had been given the following assessment upon his arrival in the frontline – 'flying training good, combat training inadequate'. It was inevitable that the 24-year-old pilot (who joined the Northern Fleet straight from flying school) would have practically no combat experience, even though he had previously served as an instructor. Strelnikov was, however, able to gain experience sortie by sortie, and this

Another pilot who claimed five victories with the Hurricane, Vasiliy Strelnikov was born in 1919 in the Krasnodar region, the son of a peasant family. After his second year at Taganrog Aviation Technical School he entered Eysk Naval Aviation School, graduating in late 1942. Strelnikov then transferred to the Northern Fleet Air Force for conversion training onto the Hurricane. Posted to 78th IAP in December 1942, he scored his first aerial victory while flying a Hurricane on 23 June 1943. On 6 May 1945 Strelnikov was awarded the title of HSU and received the Order of the Red Banner, by which time he was serving as a squadron commander

soon enabled him to become both a capable and confident commander and fighter pilot.

Strelnikov finally opened his score on 23 June. In the early hours eight 78th IAP Hurricanes, together with a similar number of P-39s from 255th IAP, took off to escort four Il-2s from 46th ShAP that had been ordered to attack an enemy convoy. The vessels were being protected by a pair of Bf 110s, and according to Strelnikov's memoirs, the twin-engined fighters immediately appeared in his field of vision as the convoy came under attack. As one of the Bf 110s passed in front of him, Strelnikov turned slightly and, catching it briefly in his sights, gave it a long burst of machine gun fire. The German aircraft began to trail smoke and went down, although this victory is unconfirmed.

Strelnikov's second claim, a Bf 109 on 20 July, was also made during an escort mission. Indeed, it was the air battle during which ace Aleksey Pilipenko was shot down and killed. Of the six Hurricanes involved only three returned, the remaining fighters being lost due to poor coordination with the accompanying P-39s. Strelnikov was one of the lucky ones.

These 78th IAP Hurricanes were photographed at a sunny Vaenga-2 airfield in the summer of 1943, each machine being equipped with a locally devised dust filter. They are also carrying a single 200-litre (44-gallon) external fuel tank beneath each wing, the additional fuel provided by these stores allowing pilots to undertake long-range attacks on enemy shipping in the Barents Sea

Now a lieutenant, he found himself in a similar situation on 14 September, again while escorting *Shturmoviks*, during his 100th combat sortie. This time the six Hurricanes were joined by four 255th IAP P-39s and eight Yak-1s from 20th IAP. They were escorting 11 attack aircraft flying in two groups, and once again targeting enemy shipping. While still en route to the target the Soviet aircraft were attacked by Bf 109s. A running battle ensued that continued over the target and during the Soviet formation's return flight. The first to engage the German fighters were the Yak-1s, and despite their best efforts, and those of the P-39 pilots, the Bf 109s were able to reach the Il-2s. However, they still had to deal with the Hurricanes of the close escort, as Vasiliy Strelnikov recalled;

'A serious air battle had begun. The whole sky was criss-crossed with tracer from bullets and shells. The first aircraft were shot down and the first parachute canopies could be seen. The German aircraft, using their numerical superiority, had begun to break through the small groups towards the formations of ground attack aircraft.

'My group went into battle and we incurred losses. One of my Il-2s was shot down. Very soon in my group only my pair remained, but I managed to take the ground attack aircraft to the point where they commenced their runs against the ships. The German convoy opened fire on them with a furious, and accurate, barrage. The German fighter pilots, now at risk from their own anti-aircraft defences, stopped pursuing the ground attack aircraft and instead headed to where the Il-2s would be completing their attack runs so as to deal with them there. I could see what the Germans were planning, so I rushed there with my wingman. After nine or ten Il-2s had completed their attacks, my wingman was shot down by a direct hit from a large-calibre shell [Jr Lt Aleksey Mashonkin was killed on his 48th combat sortie – Author]. I was now alone.

'Joining the combat formation of ground attack aircraft, I started to cover the Il-2s from the rear in conjunction with their air gunners. The environment had become much more difficult for us as there were now 19 Me 109s bearing down on the Ilyushins. I was alone. The Il-2 pilots were all experienced, and they stayed close to the water to deny the Germans an opportunity to attack from below. This made my task of countering attacks from the Me 109s rather easier.

'Having repelled another attack from an enemy fighter and then returned to my place in the formation, I noticed another German machine on its own lining up for an attack on the trailing group of Ilyushins. I came up right next to the enemy pilot, and I can clearly recall that he was wearing a grey balaclava helmet and gloves. I let him overtake me a little and then turned in behind him and hit his fighter in the starboard side using all my guns. The fighter turned over and went down. It was just like on the firing range. However, minutes later my situation took a turn for the worse.

'An Me 109 was bearing down on me and, after a series of attacks, someone scored a hit with a shell in the starboard section of the Hurricane's wing where the fuel tank was located. My fighter caught fire, forcing me to leave the ground attack aircraft and head back to the Sredniy peninsula, and our airfield, at full speed. This was very risky, but I was lucky. I flew some 80 km [50 miles] in my burning aircraft, and having reached friendly territory, I prepared to land. I opened the canopy, unfastened the harness and began to lower the undercarriage. It was only then that I fully realised just how serious the fire was.

'After the undercarriage had been lowered, the blaze spread rapidly. Flames entered the cockpit and I started to burn. I had only one option – to ditch immediately. But I had so little time, and had to do so with the undercarriage down and with no reduction in speed. As soon as the wheels touched the water, the aircraft tipped sharply

Patrol vessels of the Northern Fleet in Kola Bay. During the spring and summer of 1943, fierce air battles were fought over shipping in this bay, with Hurricane units often experiencing heavy losses at the hands of JG 5

onto its nose. I was thrown about 100 m from the cockpit, but this saved my life. This is how my final battle, and my final flight in the Hurricane, ended.'

Further interesting details about this action are contained in this Northern Fleet Air Force report, which add to Strelnikov's recollection of the engagement that almost cost him his life;

'The leading group of Hurricanes, led by Lt Strelnikov and his wingman, continued to pursue the Il-2s while repelling enemy attacks. After a short time Lt Strelnikov's wingman, Jr Lt Mashonkin, became cut off by enemy fighters, and during his manoeuvres he strayed into the firing zone of the anti-aircraft defence vessels and was shot down by heavy machine guns.

'The Il-2s were targeted by enemy fighters as they completed their attacks. Lt Strelnikov, who remained on his own, positioned himself behind the trailing pair of Il-2s and repelled enemy attacks. At a point 15-20 km [9-12 miles] from the target, Lt Strelnikov noticed a single Fw 190 that had approached the Il-2's port wingman and opened fire from a distance of 100-150 m. Strelnikov, who at that point was some 50-80 m above the Il-2s, in turn opened fire on the Fw 190. After this the enemy turned away, climbing to the left. However, with no reserves of speed, the German pilot could not get away, and he was again attacked by Strelnikov. The enemy aircraft started to emit smoke, then fell on to one wing and crashed into the sea. All the Il-2 crews witnessed the fall of the Fw 190.

'A short while later, Lt Strelnikov was attacked by two Me 109s, which succeeded in damaging his Hurricane. Manoeuvring away from the attack and escaping behind the Il-2s, gunners in the latter aircraft did not recognise the Hurricane and fired on it, setting it ablaze. Lt Strelnikov headed for Pummanki airfield in his burning aircraft, but the engine soon gave out and the pilot was forced to ditch his fighter 100 m from the shore. He was picked up by soldiers from the coastal defence batteries.'

In all, the Soviets lost four Hurricanes during this raid on the enemy convoy, and three pilots were killed – Jr Lts Grigoriy Dzheriev (103 combat sorties), Aleksey Mashonkin (48) and Ilya Kostenok (97). The attack aircraft also incurred heavy losses, with five Il-2s being shot down and three aircrew killed. It is possible that the victim of Strelnikov's close range attack was a Bf 109G-2 of 7./JG 5, its pilot, Oberfeldwebel Erich Beulich, being killed. This victory represented Strelnikov's fifth success in the Hurricane. He was awarded the Order of the Red Banner on 2 October.

His third (an Fw 190) and fourth (a Bf 109) victories had been claimed on 3 and 28 August. Strelnikov reported the Focke-

A Hurricane IIC of the Northern Fleet Air Force buzzes a Soviet naval vessel patrolling in Kola Bay

Wulf's destruction when he returned from the Kola Gulf, where he had been providing cover for patrolling vessels of the Northern Fleet that had been threatened by enemy fighter-bombers. Strelnikov was leading four Hurricanes when they encountered a similar number of enemy fighters and became embroiled in a fast-moving battle. The Soviet pilots returned to base, having suffered no losses.

Seen here, from left to right, are 78th IAP squadron commander Capt Vasiliy Pronchenko, Jr Lt Grigoriy Dzheriev and Lt Vasiliy Strelnikov. Dzheriev had claimed a solitary Hurricane victory by the time he was killed in action on 14 September 1943

The claim filed on 28 August followed a mission by eight Hurricanes, again led by Strelnikov, to an enemy airfield as part of a torpedo attack on German shipping. The mission could not be completed due to fog over the target area, but during their return flight the Hurricanes encountered eight Bf 109s, which they engaged. The ensuing battle was a ferocious one, and the German pilots succeeded in shooting down three Hurricanes. Sgts Mikhail Oganov (24 combat sorties) and Aleksey Kazankov (five) were killed, but Sgt Ivan Kondratyev (three combat sorties) managed to ditch his aircraft 30 m from the shore and was rescued.

The surviving Hurricane pilots closed up into a defensive formation and set course for friendly territory, but the German fighters continued their pursuit as far as the Rybachiy peninsula, where they broke off the chase after coming under intense anti-aircraft fire. The Soviet pilots duly reported the destruction of three enemy fighters. Apart from Strelnikov's victory, Jr Lts Viktor Kukibniy and Aleksey Mashonkin each claimed a kill – Kukibniy's fourth and Mashonkin's first. According to German records, however, only Bf 109G-2 Wk-Nr. 13618 suffered damage, and that came about when Unteroffizier Hans Vahle crash-landed at the end of the sortie. It is possible that the Messerschmitt, which was later written off, could have suffered battle damage inflicted by pilots from 78th IAP.

As previously noted by Strelnikov himself, his memorable action on 14 September was his last as a Hurricane pilot. Soon afterwards 78th IAP was pulled back to the rear to re-equip with the P-40. In March 1944, after intensive training, the regiment returned to the front, but the nature of its operations changed with its conversion to the new fighter. The P-40 was employed mainly as a fighter-bomber, attacking both

78th IAP Hurricane IIBs are prepared for their next combat mission at Vaenga-1. Note the additional external fuel tanks that were used to extend the fighters' range for attacks on enemy shipping

ground targets and shipping. Strelnikov achieved further success in this new role, and on 21 July 1944 he was made a squadron commander. All his combat successes were listed in the recommendation for his award of the title of HSU, dated 22 October. It stated;

'For the 150 combat sorties he has carried out and for the six enemy aircraft that he has personally shot down; for the two minesweepers, patrol launch, 600-ton self-propelled barge, 50-ton motorboat, 70-ton SKA motorboat, 600-ton tug and two barges that he has personally sunk; for the suppression of an enemy gun battery; for the two ammunition dumps he set on fire; for the two enemy barges he sank as part of a group; for the patrol ship and enemy launch he personally damaged; for leading the squadron which inflicted such damage on the enemy; and for the personal example of bravery, courage and heroism in air combat, he is worthy of this high governmental award.'

Vasiliy Strelnikov also received the Order of Lenin and the Order of the Red Banner three times, on 2 October 1943, 4 June 1944 and 16 October 1944. Post-war, he was awarded the Order of the October Revolution and served with Black Sea Fleet naval aviation. In March 1955 he completed courses on the development of the officer corps at the Air Force Academy and on 24 April 1975 he was awarded the title of Lieutenant General of Aviation. The title of Pilot Emeritus followed in 1981. Strelnikov died on 23 October 1993, having retained fond memories of flying the Hurricane to the end of his days. In his memoirs he had this to say of the British fighter;

'I began my service in 1940 as a graduate of the naval aviation academy and left in 1981 as a Lieutenant General of Aviation. During my years of service I became familiar with the greatest variety of aircraft types, from training biplanes to supersonic bombers. But I remember with special affection the one which was simple by today's standards – the Hurricane. It was in this very aircraft that I encountered war at a time when the combat potential of the Luftwaffe was at its zenith during the most difficult years for our country, 1942-43. I recorded victories in it and stayed alive when I was shot down. This is undoubtedly due to this rugged and reliable British aircraft.'

Vice-Admiral Vasiliy Strelnikov served as a fighter pilot flying Hurricanes in the polar region between December 1942 and December 1943, claiming five victories with the aircraft. He retained fond memories of the British fighter

APPENDICES

Soviet Hurricane Aces

Ranking	Pilot	Rank	Hero of the Soviet Union	Air Force unit/s	Hurricane victories	Total victories (individual + shared)	Number of sorties/number of air combats	Date of death in action	Date entered combat and types flown
NORTHERN FLEET AIR FORCE									
1	P G Sgibnev	major	HSU	78th IAP, 2nd GKAP	11	19	360/38	3/5/43	22/6/41 I-153, Hurricane, P-39
2	P I Orlov	captain	HSU	78th IAP, 2nd GKAP	9	12	329/32	15/3/43	18/10/42 Hurricane, P-40, P-39
3	S G Kurzenkov	captain	HSU	78th IAP, 2nd GKAP, 78th IAP	8	8	209/20		8/10/42 Hurricane
4	K K Babiy	captain		72nd SAP, 2nd GKAP, 78th IAP	7	7	?		22/6/41 I-153, Hurricane, P-40
5	A Ya Dizhevskiy	captain		72nd SAP, 78th IAP 27th IAP	7	7	?		22/6/41 I-15bis, Hurricane
6	V S Doroshin	captain		72nd SAP, 78th IAP	6	6	437/?	23/6/43	22/6/42 I-15bis, Hurricane
7	A M Pilipenko	senior lieutenant		78th IAP	6	6	221/?	20/7/43	16/4/42 Hurricane
8	D F Amosov	captain		78th IAP, 2nd GKAP, 27th IAP, 255th IAP	5	8	321/?	10/5/44	22/6/41 I-153, Hurricane, P-39
9	A A Kovalenko	major	HSU	72nd SAP, 78th IAP, 2nd GKAP	5	14	207/38		22/6/41 I-16, Hurricane, P-40
10	V P Pronchenko	captain		2nd GKAP, 78th IAP	5	5	?		16/4/42 Hurricane
11	V S Adonkin	major	HSU	72nd SAP, 27th IAP, 78th IAP, 255th IAP	5	13+7	365/42	17/3/44	22/6/41 I-153, I-16, Hurricane, P-39
12	V P Strelnikov	captain	HSU	78th IAP	5	7	150/14		12/42 Hurricane, P-40
13	V P Shalaev	captain		2nd GKAP, 78th IAP, 44th SAP, 53rd SAP	5	5	?	17/6/44	10/2/42 Hurricane, P-40
KARELIAN FRONT AIR FORCE									
	P I Gavrilov	captain		152nd IAP	5	7+3	?	22/3/43	22/6/41 I-153, Hurricane

Hurricane victories by Soviet pilots

Pilot	Rank	Hero of the Soviet Union	Air Force unit/s	Hurricane victories	Total victories (individual + shared)	Date of death in action	Types flown in combat
NORTHERN FLEET AIR FORCE							
V N Alagurov	captain		72nd SAP, 78th IAP, 2nd GKAP	4	4	11/7/44	I-153, Hurricane, P-40
E M Dilalyan	senior lieutenant		78th IAP	4	4		Hurricane
V A Kukibniy	junior lieutenant		78th IAP	4	4		Hurricane
N I Nikolaev	senior lieutenant		78th IAP	4	4		Hurricane
? ? Nour	senior lieutenant		78th IAP	4	4		Hurricane
A P Markevich	major		78th IAP, 2nd GKAP	4	4		Hurricane
Kh I Abishev	captain		72nd SAP, 78th IAP, 2nd GKAP	3	5		I-16, Hurricane, P-39
A M Avtsyn	lieutenant		78th IAP, 118th RAP	3	3	4/7/44	Hurricane, Yak-9
E V Bulat	junior lieutenant		78th IAP	3	3	29/6/43	Hurricane
N A Bokiy	senior lieutenant	HSU	72nd SAP, 78th IAP, 2nd GKAP	3	17		Hurricane, P-40, P-39
? ? Ignatyev	senior lieutenant		78th IAP	3	3		Hurricane, P-40
P L Kolomiets	captain	HSU	78th IAP, 2nd GKAP	3	13		Hurricane, P-39
S M Loginov	major		78th IAP, 2nd GKAP	3	5		Hurricane
K K Lopatin	sergeant		78th IAP	3	3	28/5/42	Hurricane
V G Mitrofanov	lieutenant		78th IAP	3	4		Hurricane
S P Podyachev	senior lieutenant		78th IAP	3	3	27/9/43	Hurricane
V P Pokrovskiy	captain	HSU	72nd SAP, 78th IAP, 2nd GKAP	3	11		I-16, Hurricane, P-40
P A Obuvalov	lieutenant		78th IAP, 2nd GKAP	3	3	28/4/42	Hurricane
A E Tulskiy	senior lieutenant		78th IAP, 255th IAP	3	4		I-15bis, Hurricane
I A Bugakov	junior lieutenant		78th IAP	2	2		Hurricane
M N Verevkin	captain		72nd SAP, 27th IAP, 78th IAP	2	3	11/5/44	I-15bis, I-153, Hurricane, P-40
E T Dzhykaev	lieutenant		78th IAP	2	2	12/5/42	Hurricane
I S Edush	senior lieutenant		27th IAP	2	3	12/10/44	Hurricane, P-40, P-39
V I Kirichenko	lieutenant		78th IAP	2	5		Hurricane, P-40
I I Kostenok	junior lieutenant		78th IAP	2	2	14/9/43	Hurricane
F M Kochanov	junior lieutenant		78th IAP	2	2		Hurricane
V V Kravchenko	senior lieutenant		78th IAP, 2nd GKAP	2	4	10/5/42	I-16, Hurricane
A A Krasilnikov	captain		27th IAP	2	2+1		I-15bis, Hurricane, P-40, P-39
V I Laptev	senior lieutenant		27th IAP	2	2	10/10/44	Hurricane, P-40, P-39
I Ya Popovich	senior lieutenant		78th IAP, 118th RAP	2	2		Hurricane, Spitfire
D A Reutov	captain		72nd SAP, 78th IAP, 2nd GKAP	2	3	26/12/42	I-15bis, Hurricane, P-40
T F Chistov	junior lieutenant		27th IAP, 255th IAP	2	2	23/4/44	Hurricane, P-39
B F Safonov	lieutenant colonel	twice HSU	72nd SAP, 78th IAP, 2nd GKAP	2	20+6	30/5/42	I-16, Hurricane, P-40
V A Ageychev	captain		27th IAP	1	3	25/6/43	I-16, Hurricane
V M Averyanov	junior lieutenant		78th IAP	1	1	18/8/43	Hurricane
? ? Bershanskiy	senior lieutenant		78th IAP	1	1		Hurricane
P D Bogdanov	lieutenant		27th IAP	1	1		Hurricane
M G Volkov	lieutenant		78th IAP	1	1	17/12/41	Hurricane
G L Dzheriev	junior lieutenant		78th IAP	1	1	14/9/43	Hurricane
E A Evstigneev	sergeant		78th IAP	1	1	10/5/42	Hurricane
B G Ermilin	lieutenant		27th IAP	1	2		Hurricane, P-40, P-39

L V Zhdanov	captain		72nd SAP, 78th IAP	1	1		I-153, Hurricane
I L Zhivotovskiy	senior lieutenant		72nd SAP, 78th IAP	1	2	10/5/42	Hurricane
N G Kascheev	junior lieutenant		78th IAP	1	1		Hurricane
N I Kirillov	junior lieutenant		78th IAP	1	1		Hurricane
N K Kravchenko	lieutenant		78th IAP	1	2		Hurricane, P-40
P I Markov	senior lieutenant		78th IAP	1	1	16/1/43	Hurricane
? ? Mashonkin	junior lieutenant		78th IAP	1	1		Hurricane
V A. Nazarov	senior sergeant		78th IAP	1	1	27/5/42	Hurricane
S I Pankrashin	lieutenant		78th IAP, 118th RAP	1	1		Hurricane, Yak-9
P D Romanov	sergeant major		78th IAP, 2nd GKAP	1	5		I-16, Hurricane, P-39
P I Savitskiy	junior lieutenant		27th IAP	1	1	5/6/43	Hurricane

KARELIAN FRONT AIR FORCE**

V A Basov	captain		152nd IAP	3	5+1		I-153, Hurricane, P-40
S P Zelentsov	junior lieutenant		152nd IAP	3	?		Hurricane, P-40
P G Zubach	sergeant major		760th IAP	3	3+3		Hurricane, P-40
? ? Polyga	junior lieutenant		17th GShAP	3	3+1		Hurricane
N A Sinitsyn	sergeant major		760th IAP	3	3+1	8/3/43	Hurricane
V N Faerman	captain		152nd IAP	3	3	21/4/43	I-153, Hurricane, P-40
P N Eliseev	major		152nd IAP	2	2		Hurricane
F G Zadorozhniy	senior lieutenant		152nd IAP	2	2	21/6/42	Hurricane
A I Nikolaenkov	senior lieutenant	HSU	126th, 42nd, 760th IAP	2	8+23	7/6/43	I-16, MiG-3, Hurricane, P-40
N D. Sklyarenko	major		147th, 760th IAP	2	?		I-153, Hurricane, P-40
V A Andreev	lieutenant		147th, 760th IAP	1	1	15/3/42	I-15bis, Hurricane
V M Arakhovskiy	senior lieutenant		147th, 760th IAP	1	?+4		I-153, Hurricane
E I Arefyev	junior lieutenant		760th IAP	1	?		
A I Bazarov	sergeant		760th IAP	1*	1	17/5/42	
F D Bobrovnik	senior lieutenant		760th IAP	1	1		
V A Bogatykh	lieutenant		152nd IAP	1	3		Hurricane, P-40
A V Budnikov	sergeant		760th IAP	1	1		
? ? Evdokimov	junior lieutenant		17th GShAP	1	1		Hurricane
L A Evtyushenko	sergeant		760th IAP	1	1	21/2/43	
A E Zhgun	senior lieutenant		147th, 760th IAP	1	2+5	17/3/42	I-153, Hurricane
G I Zhmurko	senior lieutenant		152nd IAP	1	1		Hurricane
S G. Ivanov	lieutenant		152nd IAP	1	2+1		I-153, Hurricane
N A Knyazev	senior sergeant		152nd IAP	1	1		Hurricane
V I Korolev	captain	HSU	147th, 760th IAP	1	2+10		I-153, Hurricane, P-40
V I Krupskiy	captain	HSU	147th, 760th IAP, 20th GIAP	1	9+10		I-153, Hurricane, P-40
V N Lyusov	lieutenant		152nd IAP	1	1	9/1/42	Hurricane
I M Orlov	sergeant major		760th IAP	1	1	6/3/43	Hurricane
N A Prokofyev	senior lieutenant		145th, 760th IAP	1	1+8		I-16, MiG-3, Hurricane, P-40
D G Polyakov	lieutenant		760th IAP	1	1+6	24/4/42	Hurricane
N F Repnikov	senior lieutenant		152nd IAP	1*	2	4/12/41	I-153, Hurricane
M N Ryabcheko	junior lieutenant		20th GIAP, 152nd IAP	1	1		Hurricane, P-40
I I Serdyuchenko	senior lieutenant		152nd IAP	1	1		I-153, Hurricane
I S Snig	junior lieutenant		760th IAP	1	3+7	17/11/42	Hurricane, P-40
A V Sorokin	senior lieutenant		152nd IAP	1	1	30/3/42	I-153, Hurricane

122ND IAD OF THE AIR DEFENCE FORCES***

G D Ogoltsov	lieutenant		769th IAP	3	3+3	29/7/42	Hurricane
N M Chagin	senior political leader		769th IAP	3	3+3		Hurricane
V P Znamenskiy	senior lieutenant		767th IAP	2	2+9		Hurricane, Yak-7B
G I Kozlov	captain		65th ShAP, 767th, 768th IAP	2	4+4		I-15bis, Hurricane, P-40, Yak-9
V A Nizhnik	senior lieutenant		769th IAP	2	2+10		Hurricane, P-40
S G Ivanov	captain		769th IAP	1	1+5		Hurricane, P-40, Yak-9
L A Anokhin	senior political leader		769th IAP	1	1+4		Hurricane

S F Kramor	sergeant	769th IAP	1	1+2	29/7/42	Hurricane
N F Aksinin	sergeant major	769th IAP	1	1	12/7/42	Hurricane
P N Bardash	senior lieutenant	768th IAP	1	1+4		Hurricane
A I Bezhentsev	senior lieutenant	966th IAP	1	1+1		Hurricane
A G Borisov	major	768th, 966th IAP	1	1+5		Hurricane, P-40
V I Gavrilov	senior lieutenant	768th, 769th IAP	1	3+15		Hurricane, P-40, Yak-7B
N S Dygalo	sergeant major	769th IAP	1	1+1	25/4/43	Hurricane
I G Zakharenkov	senior lieutenant	966th IAP	1	1		Hurricane
N E Zubkov	senior sergeant	767th IAP	1	1		Hurricane, Yak-9
P N Eliseev	major	769th IAP	1	?		Hurricane, P-40
I F Krasnov	lieutenant	769th IAP	1	1+6		Hurricane
S P Negulyaev	junior lieutenant	769th IAP	1*	1+1	23/4/42	Hurricane
N Ya Nikulin	senior lieutenant	966th IAP	1	1		Hurricane
? ? Pavlov	senior lieutenant	768th IAP	1	1		Hurricane
P I Plekhanov	senior lieutenant	767th IAP	1	1+3	7/4/44	Hurricane, P-40, Yak-7B
N G Polkovnikov	senior sergeant	966th IAP	1	1	16/3/43	Hurricane
S I Proshakov	senior lieutenant	966th IAP	1	1	13/4/43	Hurricane
M G Shmyrin	captain	768th IAP	1	2+8		Hurricane, P-40

Notes

*ramming attack

** No records of the victories achieved by Hurricane pilots serving with 197th, 435th, 609th, 835th and 837th IAPs of the Karelian Front Air Force have been found. The records of Karelian Front Air Force fighter regiments list both individual and shared victories. Shared victories were usually attributed to all members of the participating group. They were not shared as fractions, which meant that some pilots appeared to have achieved particularly high scores. 760th IAP's Snr Lt A I Nikolaenkov, for example, is listed as having scored eight individual and 23 shared kills. The financial reward for shooting down an enemy aircraft was shared evenly between the pilots in the group concerned. In an engagement on 21 February 1942, for example, the pilots of 760th IAP (Capt Korolev, Snr Lts Zhgun and Krupskiy, Lts Nikolaenkov and Polyakov and Snr Sgt Snig) reported that they had shot down four Bf 109s. The total award for four aircraft shot down, 4000 roubles, was shared between them, with each pilot receiving 666 roubles

*** Victories attributed to 122nd IAD pilots are based on operational reports, so the number of shared victories is not clear, as in some cases not all the names of the participants in a particular combat were given

HURRICANE AIRFIELDS

Airfield	Period	Unit
Northern Fleet Air Force		
Vaenga-1/2	10/41 to 10/43	2nd GKAP, 78th IAP
Kildin	5-12/43	27th IAP
Pummanki	6-11/43	one squadron of 78th IAP
122nd IAD of the Air Defence Forces		
Arktika	3/42 to 1/44	767th and 768th IAP
Shonguy	1/42 to 4/44	768th and 769th IAP
Rosta	2-7/43	769th IAP (periodically)
Beloe More	1-9/43	966th IAP
*7th Air Army (Karelian Front Air Force)**		
Afrikanda	5-11/42	609th IAP
Murmashi	1-5/42	147th IAP, later 20th GIAP
Beloe More	1-4/42	760th IAP
	5-12/42	435th IAP
Boyarskaya	5/42 to 11/43	760th IAP
Gremyakha	7/42 to 12/42	835th IAP
	3-7/43	152nd IAP
Kirovsk	5-8/42	197th and 837th IAP
Loukhi-13km	1-4/42	145th IAP
	12/42 to 12/43	435th IAP
Letnyaya	11/41 to 4/42	152nd IAP
Poduzhemye	3-4/42	767th IAP
	4-12/42	17th GShAP
Polyarniy Krug	7-11/43	152nd IAP
Segezha	1-4/42	609th IAP
	4/42 to 2/43	152nd IAP

* 7th Air Army regiments could be temporarily based at any of the following airfields for two to three weeks, and this mostly affected 145th (later 19th GIAP), 152nd, 609th and 760th IAP and 17th GShAP

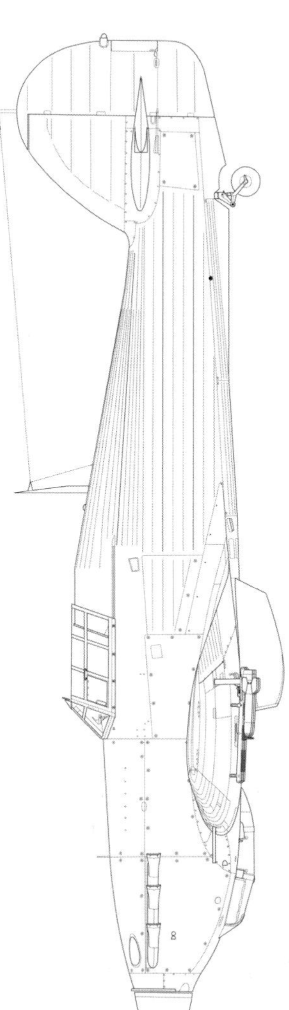

0 metres 1 2

0 feet 3 6

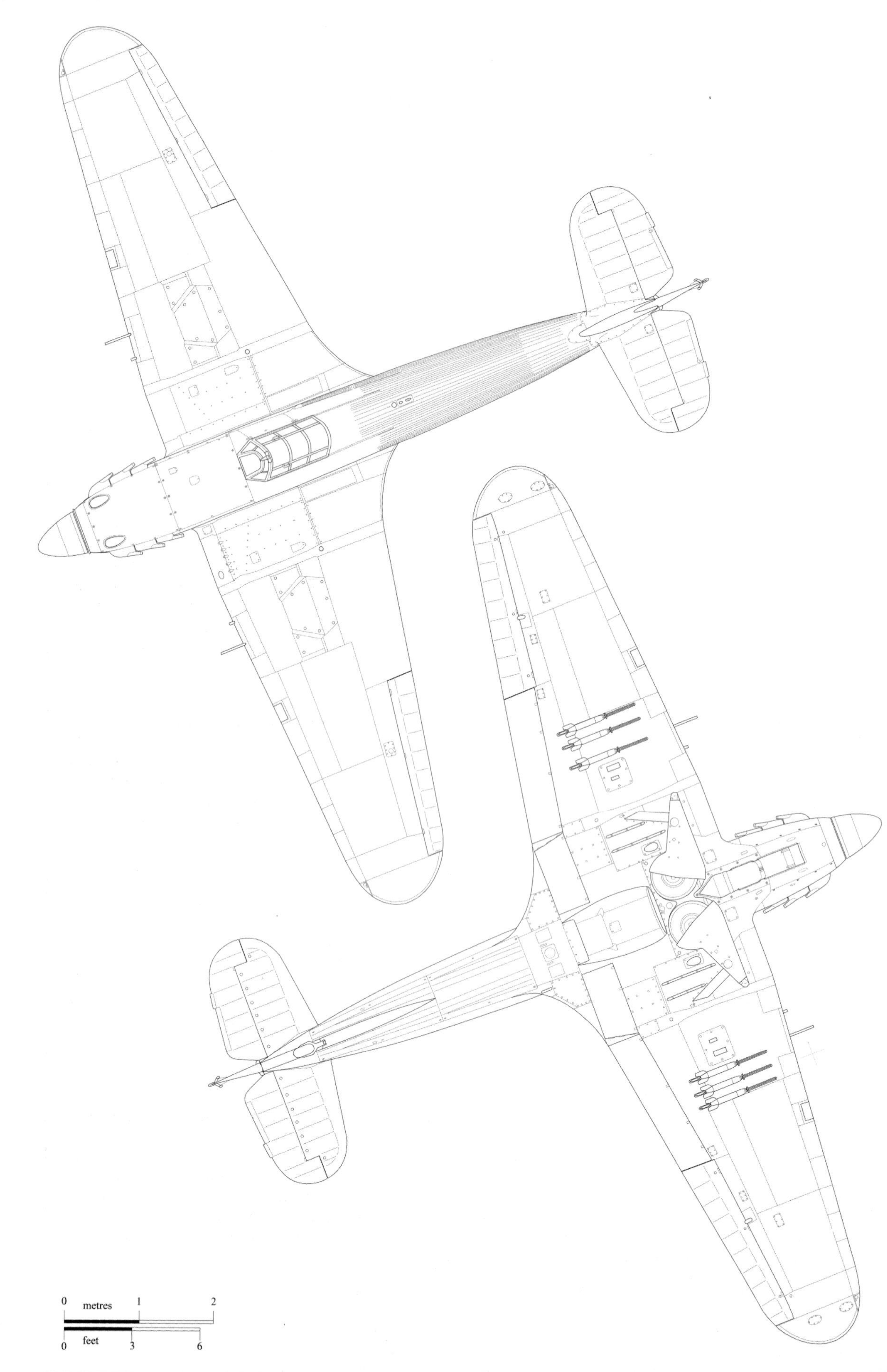

0
metres
1
2
feet
3
6

Colour Plates

1
Hurricane IIB Z5205 of No 134 Sqn, No 151 Wing, Vaenga-1, October 1941
This aircraft was flown by Battle of Britain veteran Sqn Ldr A G Miller, CO of No 134 Sqn, who was awarded the Order of Lenin for service in the polar region of the Soviet Union. In October 1941 the fighter was transferred to the newly re-established 78th IAP of the Northern Fleet Air Force at Vaenga-1.

2
Hurricane IIB Z5205 of 78th IAP, Northern Fleet Air Force, Vaenga-2, late 1941
After Z5205's transfer by No 151 Wing to 78th IAP it was allocated to the unit commander, and ace, Capt Boris Safonov. The aircraft sustained engine failure during aerial combat on 17 December 1941 and Safonov was forced to make an emergency landing on a frozen lake, where it was destroyed by German fighters in series of strafing attacks on 11 January 1942. The ranking ace of the Northern Fleet Air Force, Safonov shot down 20 enemy aircraft, two of them – on 17 (in Z5205) and 31 December 1941 – while flying a Hurricane.

3
Hurricane IIB Z3768 of No 81 Sqn, No 151 Wing, Vaenga-1, autumn 1941
This aircraft arrived at Archangelsk in September 1941, after which it was assembled and test flown at Kegostrov airfield before being ferried to Vaenga-1 airfield near Murmansk. Flown by Sgt Crewe on several operational sorties, the fighter was transferred to the re-formed 78th IAP of the Northern Fleet Air Force in October.

4
Hurricane IIB Z3768 of 78th IAP, Northern Fleet Air Force, Vaenga-2, 1941-42
This fighter was initially flown by the commander of the 3rd Wing, 3rd Squadron of 78th IAP, Lt D F Amosov. From March 1942, Z3768 was on the strength of 2nd GKAP, but it was eventually written off as a combat loss on 31 August 1942. By that time Dmitriy Amosov's score had reached seven kills, including five while in the Hurricane. The inscription applied to the fuselage of the aircraft reads 'For the All-Union Communist Party of Bolsheviks'.

5
Hurricane Z5252 of 78th IAP, Northern Fleet Air Force, Vaenga-2, October 1941
This Hurricane was transferred from No 151 Wing's No 81 Sqn to 78th IAP, where it was flown by the commanding officer of the Northern Fleet Air Force, Maj Gen A A Kuznetsov. The fighter was subsequently passed on to 2nd GKAP, where it was modified to allow it to carry RS-82 rocket projectiles. Z5252 was shot down on 2 June 1942 while being flown by Guards Lt Pavel I Markov, who managed to make a forced landing on the surface of a frozen lake. The Hurricane soon fell through the ice and sank. Minutes prior to being shot down, Lt Markov had claimed his first combat victory when he destroyed a Bf 109. Later killed in a flying accident on 16 January 1943, Markov had by then claimed two enemy aircraft destroyed.

6
Hurricane IIB BN297 of 78th IAP, Northern Fleet Air Force, Vaenga-2, spring/summer 1942
BN297 was lost during an engagement with enemy aircraft on 22 August 1943 near the Finnish airfield of Luostari. The fighter is depicted here as it appeared during the spring and summer of 1942, when it was regularly flown by Northern Fleet ace Snr Lt Petr Sgibnev.

7
Hurricane II Z3458 of 78th IAP, Northern Fleet Air Force, Vaenga-2, June 1943
Z3458 was one of only a handful of Mk IIAs to survive in Soviet service through to 1944. Delivered to the RAF on 2 January 1941, it served with No 71 'Eagle' Sqn and No 615 Sqn Royal Auxiliary Air Force, before being transferred to the Soviet Union in March 1942. Assigned to the Northern Fleet Air Force, the fighter was flown by 2nd GKAP and 78th and 27th IAPs. Following almost four years of operational service, Z3458 was grounded on 1 November 1944 and scrapped. The aircraft is depicted here as it appeared during its time with 78th IAP in June 1943, when it was flown by Northern Fleet Hurricane ace Capt Vasiliy Adonkin.

8
Hurricane IIB HW370 of 78th IAP, Northern Fleet Air Force, Vaenga-2, spring 1943
This Hurricane was delivered to the Northern Fleet Air Force in February 1943, and it was written off three months later (on 30 May) when its pilot, Snr Sgt I A Bugakov, crashed whilst taking off from Vaenga-1. He was able to walk away from the accident unhurt.

9
Hurricane IIB KX333 of 78th IAP, Northern Fleet Air Force, Vaenga-2, May 1943
This fighter had been on the strength of the Northern Fleet Air Force for two months when, on 22 May 1943, it was written off following engine failure in flight. Its pilot, Jr Lt N T Starosvetskiy, suffered injuries during the crash-landing. Note that the aircraft is equipped with a modified sand filter and Soviet armament in the form of two ShVAK 20 mm cannon and two 12.7 mm UB machine guns in the wings.

10
Hurricane IIB JS280 of 78th IAP, Northern Fleet Air Force, Vaenga-2, 1943
This Hurricane was delivered to the Northern Fleet Air Force in March 1943 and initially assigned to 78th IAP. Seen here fitted with long-range drop tanks, a sand filter and Soviet armament, the aircraft was subsequently transferred to 27th IAP. JS280 was still serving with this unit when it was lost in combat in May 1944.

11

Hurricane IIB BD863 of 78th IAP, Northern Fleet Air Force, Vaenga-2, summer 1943

This fighter was transferred to 78th IAP from the Baltic Fleet Air Force, where it had served with 3rd GIAP, in the summer of 1943. When sent to the repair workshops for an overhaul in September of that same year it was declared a write-off due to its battle-weary condition.

12

Hurricane IIC KX452 of 78th IAP, Northern Fleet Air Force, Vaenga-2, spring 1943

This aircraft served for only a matter of weeks with 78th IAP before it was written off. Arriving at Vaenga-1 in March 1943, the 20 mm cannon-armed fighter was shot down in combat with enemy aircraft on 15 April. Its pilot, Snr Sgt I A Mikhailyuk, was severely wounded in the engagement, but he still managed to bail out.

13

Hurricane IIC KX471 of 78th IAP, Northern Fleet Air Force, Vaenga-2, summer 1943

Also cannon-armed, KX471 was destroyed on 17 July 1943 when Snr Lt A M Avtsyn crashed shortly after takeoff. Despite this setback, Aron Avtsyn continued flying Hurricanes, and had shot down three Bf 109s by the end of 1943. He was killed on 4 July 1944 while flying a Yak-7 with 118th Reconnaissance Air Regiment of the Northern Fleet Air Force.

14

Hurricane IIB of 2nd GKAP, Northern Fleet Air Force, Vaenga-2, summer 1942

The original RAF serial number of this aircraft was painted over during numerous repairs. Note that it has also been fitted with Soviet armament.

15

Hurricane IIB Z2585 of 152nd IAP, 103rd SAD, Karelian Front Air Force, Boyarskaya, February 1942

This aircraft was captured by the Finns when, on 4 February 1942, its pilot Lt F G Zadorozhniy suffered engine failure after aerial combat and had to make a forced landing in enemy territory. The pilot managed to escape and returned to his unit, while the Hurricane was repaired and impressed into service with the Finnish Air Force on 16 March 1944. Allocated the Finnish serial number HC-45, it was briefly used for training purposes until permanently grounded on 31 May 1944. Originally delivered to the RAF in early 1941, Z2585 had flown with Nos 56 and 316 Sqns prior to being sent to the USSR.

16 and 17

Hurricane IIB BM959 of 609th IAP, Karelian Front Air Force, USSR, April 1942

This aircraft was shot down during an engagement with Finnish Buffaloes of LeLv 24 on 6 April 1942 in the Rugozero area. BM959's pilot, Jr Lt N A Belitskiy, made a forced landing in enemy territory and was captured. Note different markings displayed on each side of the fuselage, with 'For the Motherland' on the port side and 'For Stalin' to starboard. Also an ex-RAF machine, this aircraft had been shipped to the USSR in December 1941.

18

Hurricane IIB BH250 of 17th GShAP, Karelian Front Air Force, USSR, summer 1942

This aircraft was on the strength of the Karelian Front Air Force from April 1942, being assigned initially to 17th GShAP. Transferred to 760th IAP seven months later, it operated mainly on the southern flank of the Karelian Front. On 5 October 1943 the veteran fighter made a belly landing after suffering engine failure, and it was broken up for spares on the 19th of that same month.

19

Hurricane IIC BN687 of 760th IAP, Karelian Front Air Force, USSR, 1942-43

Fitted with Soviet armament, this machine was used during 1942-43 to perform defensive patrols over the vital Kirov railway line. It survived several belly landings during this period and was eventually transferred to the 9th Detached Training Air Regiment in January 1944, where it was written off after yet another incident.

20

Hurricane IIB Z2751 of 147th IAP, 14th Army Air Force, Murmashi, February 1942

This unusually camouflaged aircraft served with 147th IAP on the Karelian Front during the winter of 1941-42, being based at Murmashi airfield near Murmansk. On 13 February 1942 it crashed while taking off from here, its pilot, Sgt V A Morgunov, being killed.

21

Hurricane IIB Z3326 of 147th IAP, 14th Army Air Force, Murmashi, February 1942

This aircraft was also destroyed shortly after taking off from Murmashi, Z3326 suffering engine failure on 3 February 1942. Its pilot, Sgt Maj S N Volkov, survived the crash with serious injuries.

22

Hurricane IIB BN668 of 837th IAP, 14th Army Air Force, Murmashi, September 1942

In the autumn of 1942, 837th IAP was based at Murmashi airfield, near Murmansk, and on 15 September this Hurricane fell victim to Bf 109s from 6./JG 5 *Eismeer*. Although BN668 was shot down in flames, its pilot, Sgt Maj V A Bishutin, was able to bail out of the burning fighter.

23

Hurricane IIB AP570 of 767th IAP, 122nd IAD, Air Defence Force, Arktika, summer 1942

This Hurricane was flown by 767th IAP from Arktika airfield, near Murmansk, during the summer months of 1942. It was routinely used by Sgt Maj V P Znamenskiy, who was credited with two individual and at least five shared Hurricane victories (some of them in this aircraft).

24

Hurricane IIB AP569 of 767th IAP, 122nd IAD, Air Defence Force, Arktika, May 1942

On 26 May 1942 this aircraft was crash-landed at 767th IAP's base at Arktika airfield by regimental navigation officer Capt V P

Yanchevskiy. Although AP569 had sustained only light damage, the aircraft was written off and used as a spares source.

25

Hurricane IIB Z3312 of 767th IAP, 122nd IAD, Air Defence Force, Arktika, May 1942

Lt V S Koshelev was flying this Hurricane when it too crash-landed at Arktika airfield on 26 May 1942. Like AP569, Z3312 was also dismantled for spares.

26

Hurricane IIB BE558 of 767th IAP, 122nd IAD, Air Defence Force, Poduzhemye, April 1942

On 7 April 1942 this aircraft, piloted by 767th IAP's regimental commander, Maj L P Yuryev, took off from Poduzhemye airfield in the southern sector of the Karelian Front with a groundcrewman still on the fighter's tail. The latter had been weighing the aircraft down during ground power runs. Upon realising what had happened, the pilot hastily attempted to make a turn in order to land, but the aircraft stalled and crashed due to the shift in its centre of gravity. Yuryev was killed and the groundcrewman badly injured.

27

Hurricane IIB Z3227 of 767th IAP, 122nd IAD, Air Defence Force, Poduzhemye, March 1942

Veteran Hurricane Z3227 is depicted here in the colour scheme it wore after it had been relegated from frontline duties to the role of training aircraft for new pilots assigned to 767th IAP at Poduzhemye airfield on the Karelian Front. On 21 March 1942 the aircraft crashed on landing whilst being flown by a recent arrival. The fighter was subsequently written off.

28

Hurricane IIB AP671 of 768th IAP, 122nd IAD, Air Defence Force, Arktika, spring 1942

This aircraft participated in the defence of Murmansk during the spring of 1942, being flown by 768th IAP from Arktika airfield, south of the port city.

29

Hurricane IIB Z3030 of 769th IAP, 122nd IAD, Air Defence Force, Shonguy, March 1942

This Hurricane suffered a crash landing at the 769th IAP's base at Shonguy airfield, south of Murmansk, on 20 March 1942. It was sent to a repair workshop for rebuilding but was eventually written off on 22 June due to its age.

30

Hurricane IIB BN416 of 769th IAP, 122nd IAD, Air Defence Force, Poduzhemye, April 1942

Yet another Hurricane to be badly damaged in a crash-landing during the early spring of 1942, BN416 was declared a write-off and broken up for spare parts following an incident at Poduzhemye on 2 April.

31

Hurricane IIB BG933 of 769th IAP, 122nd IAD, Air Defence Force, Arktika, July 1942

This fighter was regularly flown by Sgt S F Kramor prior to his death in aerial combat on 29 July 1942. Kramor's score at the time of his demise was one enemy aircraft shot down and two shared destroyed.

32

Hurricane IIB Z5689 of 730th IAP, 104th IAD, Air Defence Force, Kegostrov, February 1942

This Hurricane was operated by 730th IAP when the unit was based at Kegostrov airfield, near Arkhangelsk. It is illustrated here in a temporary winter scheme as it appeared during a series of training flights made in February 1942. The units of 104th IAD provided not only air cover for Arkhangelsk and its sea port, but also participated in missions to protect Allied convoys from attack by Luftwaffe dive-bombers.

INDEX

References to illustrations are shown in **bold**. Plates are shown with page and caption locators in brackets.